WHAT AM I WORTH?

WHAT AM I WORTH?

Marion Daniel

New Wine Press

New Wine Ministries
PO Box 17
Chichester
West Sussex
United Kingdom
PO19 2AW

Unless otherwise stated, all Scripture quotations are taken from The Holy
Bible, King James Version, public domain.

The Amplified Bible, Copyright © 1954, 1958, 1962, 1964, 1965, 1987 by
The Lockman Foundation.

ISBN 978-1-905991-58-7

Typeset by **documen**, www.documen.co.uk
Cover design by CCD, www.ccdgroup.co.uk
Printed in the United Kingdom

CONTENTS

DEDICATION

To my parents who gave me self-worth, and when my life shattered like a plate glass window they were still there for me and helped pick up the pieces, directing me to the One who would give me TRUE SELF-WORTH 'in HIM' forever.

INTRODUCTION

In recent years the issue of "self-worth" has been spoken about increasingly by the media and by individuals in everyday life. In an age where people frequently suffer from identity crises, it has become just as much a crime to rob someone of their self-worth as it has to assault them. People are concerned about protecting whatever self-worth they have. A simple Google search for the phrase "self-worth" brings up a list of almost 70 million web pages. This fact alone tells us that people are constantly thinking about whether or not they have value as a person and wondering how they can achieve feelings of self worth and esteem.

God, who made us, knows we will function more fully if we have self-worth. Even the world's psychologists have the theory that human needs (seen in a triangle) would put our basic needs for survival, breathing, food, water and sleep at the bottom of the triangle and at the top our needs concerned with personality and spirituality: esteem and self-actualisation. In other words, beyond our basic physiological needs, we are searching for self worth! We all need a sense of identity that places value upon us as a person. We are all searching to find our purpose and meaning in life. We all want to answer the question: *who am I and what am I here for?*

A dictionary definition of the term "self-worth" describes it as "one's worth as a person, as perceived by oneself." The distinction "as perceived by oneself" is an important one and a theme that we will return to constantly throughout this book. But to begin with, I want to ask a few questions:

What does self-worth mean to you?

Have you ever paused to ask yourself the question, "Where does my self-worth come from?"

Do you think you could get more out of life if you better understood the answers to the questions above?

How different would your life look if you truly understood your worth as a person?

As we progress through this book, I believe that you will be surprised to learn that there are many issues in our lives that have at their root a lack of self-worth. Some will be obvious, but others will not be. If anything, this is simply a reflection of the fact that we are complex beings and often it is difficult to get to the bottom of why we do the things we do. My hope is that this book will help you to take an honest and open look at yourself in order to discover what makes you tick. But more than that, I hope you begin to see yourself in the light of God's love and grace, which He has for you in great abundance.

Marion Daniel~
August 2010

GLOSSARY OF TERMS

Perhaps it is a new idea for you to look at this topic in the light of the Holy Bible. It will be simple if we take a look at some of the words that will appear through the pages of this book.

God: The One who made us and is in charge of our lives if we ask Him to be!

Jesus Christ: God's Son who has given His life for us on the cross that we might know God as our personal Saviour.

Holy Ghost: (Also called Holy Spirit). God's Spirit who dwells in us and releases His power through us on the earth.

Body of Christ: The family of believers who live here on earth who have the opportunity to function together for the Heavenly Father.

Holy Bible: (Also called the Word of God). Christians believe that this book is our handbook for life just as a new model of car has a handbook to show us how to get the best out of it. The Holy Word of God is inspired by God and is intended to edify our lives, not to make them more difficult.

Enemy: (Also called the devil). The spiritual foe of darkness we fight against in our everyday lives.

PART ONE

WHERE DOES A LACK OF SELF-WORTH COME FROM?

CHAPTER 1

FACTORS THAT SHAPE OUR SELF-WORTH

The definition of the word "worth" is "the quality that renders something desirable, valuable or useful". So when we speak about a person's worth or value, we are really speaking about the same thing. Our worth as individuals is the sum of all that we perceive about ourselves and how we believe other people see us. Neither of these sets of beliefs may correspond to how God sees us as an individual, but more on that later!

These perceptions and beliefs tend to have quite dramatic effects on our personality. Do you consider yourself to be "useful"? In life we place value upon things that are useful because they help us to accomplish things. Do you consider yourself to be "valuable"? Something that is valuable to us can be so because it is of the highest quality, or it can be valuable to us because it represents someone or something that we love a great deal. Ask yourself these questions now and reflect on the answers for a while:

How useful and valuable am I to others?

How does that make me feel?

When something is considered to be worth-*less* it means that it is basically neither useful or valuable, having no merit and being good for nothing. No one would ever want to feel like that, would they! So, why do so many people feel a sense of despair and loneliness, claiming that they feel "worthless"?

Where does such a lack of self-worth come from?

The Things that Shape our Self-Worth

In order to understand this, we first need to look at the factors that *shape* our self-worth. What are the influences that determine our perceived level of usefulness and value in our own eyes?

There are a number of possibilities.

1. The world

By "the world" I mean the influence of society and the social norms and patterns of life that dominate our thinking. The media is a great influencer in society, since we cannot escape its constant barrage of images and messages. And the media is prone to continually associate self-worth with such things as our image, our body, our achievements in life, our success etc. Therefore it sets an unsafe foundation for building our self-worth upon.

2. Parents, family and friends

We are influenced perhaps most profoundly by our parents and our peers (whether they be our siblings or our friends). How we came into the world and how we were raised by our parents deeply affects our self-worth. Our childhood is the phase of our lives when our beliefs about the nature of life, what we believe about ourselves, what others think of us etc, are instilled and ingrained into us – either directly and deliberately, or indirectly and accidentally. How our parents interacted with us, spoke to us, spoke about us – all these factors will have shaped our thinking and ultimately our inherent sense of value.

3. *Our environment*

Closely allied to the influence of our parents and peers is that of our environment. The circumstances into which we were born and raised will have had an effect on our self-worth. If, for instance, we were born into a poor family that struggled financially, that will have affected us, maybe to the extent that we tend to feel insecure and worry constantly about having enough to live on. We may feel that we personally have something to prove with an attitude that says, "I'm better than this." In other words, having been raised in this environment may cause us to strive to prove that we are worth more than our background and circumstances might suggest.

Others, who were born into privileged circumstances may not feel a lack of worth in the same way, but they will, of course, struggle in other areas. Perhaps because of their privileged start in life they also have something to prove – that they are good enough to succeed on their own, without their parents' help? Self-worth is a very complex issue.

4. *Our lifestyle*

Many people's self-worth is entirely wrapped up in their lifestyle. If all of that is suddenly stripped away then, people can be left with a serious identity crisis on their hands. Although Father God never uses such criteria as our lifestyle to establish our self-worth, society uses it all the time. Society wants to know,

How much money have you got?

How big is your house and what is it worth?

15

Where do you take your holidays?

What kind of car do you drive?

What kind of clothes do you wear?

Society attributes value to individuals based on such criteria, but what is interesting (and alarming) is that none of these criteria tells us anything about a person – whether they are morally good, kind, generous, gracious or, conversely, immoral, mean or corrupt. The trappings of lifestyle actually yield no information whatsoever about the characteristics that give a person worth! As believers, we need the wisdom of our Heavenly Father to see beyond everything that is external and superficial and not judge people according to their lifestyle.

5. *Our status*

Closely linked to the trappings of lifestyle is our status in life – another factor that will determine how we feel about ourselves, not least because "status" is another of society's benchmarks to attribute worth, value and usefulness to a person.

Do we have a title?

Do we have letters after our name?

Have we been promoted in our job to a position of responsibility and authority?

Better still, do we run our own successful business? Or alternatively, do we hold some respected position in society that gives us status? Perhaps we have become a local MP? Maybe a magistrate? Maybe we are a respected member of some local club?

The idea of achieving status in life is one that tries to suck us all in at one time or another and often we find ourselves being squeezed into its mould. The trouble is, if for whatever reason we don't achieve a reasonable level of status compared to our peers then we can end up feeling rejected and consequently have very low self-esteem.

6. *Our image*

For many, the media is the most instrumental factor in determining their self-worth because they constantly look to it in order to inform their sense of image. Although we know only too well that the images portrayed by the media which tell us, "This is how to look cool or sensual or successful", are a gross misrepresentation of reality, it is amazing how we are still influenced by them! If the images that the media constantly beams into our homes are of no consequence, as some advertisers claim, then why is there such a high incidence of anorexia and bulimia in teenage girls who are desperate to look as thin as a "supermodel"? Or why do companies use popular celebrities to promote their products?

The fact is, we are constantly looking at the "world's-eye" view of self-image and constantly examining ourselves to see how we measure up to it. Thankfully, Father God uses different criteria to attribute worth to us! He has completely different ideas about our worth and it is not based on any of the six items above. Later we will look in more detail at how God sees us and how we are to view ourselves as a consequence.

Being blind to the light of the Gospel means
that not only are unbelievers ignorant of
Jesus – of who He is and what He has done
for us – but they are also ignorant of the

*whole spectrum of God's truth as revealed
in Scripture. As a result they know nothing
about how God views their worth.*

Why Is Our Self-Worth Shaped By These Things?

How is it that people, often unconsciously, find themselves being squeezed and moulded by these factors that often lead to a lack of self-worth and value? We may look for many reasons and come up with many answers. I've already mentioned the media twice above, but ultimately I don't believe it is the media's fault. The root cause is a spiritual one.

The Apostle Paul writes in his second letter to the Corinthian church,

*"But if our gospel be hid, it is hid to them that are lost:
In whom the god of this world hath blinded the minds
of them which believe not, lest the light of the glorious
gospel of Christ, who is the image of God, should shine
unto them."*

(2 CORINTHIANS 4:3-4)

This verse speaks about the fact that our enemy, the devil, employs a strategy of blinding the minds of those who do not know Jesus. Being blind to the light of the Gospel means that not only are unbelievers ignorant of Jesus – of who He is and what He has done for us – but they are also ignorant of the whole spectrum of God's truth as revealed in Scripture. As a result they know nothing about how God views their worth. They judge themselves and their value based on society's warped and distorted criteria, which will ultimately lead to a lack of self-worth when they don't make the grade.

18

This verse implies that when we come to Christ, the Saviour, the veil is lifted and at last we begin to see things as they really are – the superficiality and shallowness of the world's view and the depth and quality of the truth of the Father. This is certainly true regarding the issues of salvation and life and death. But once we are saved we have to go through a process of transformation (the Bible calls this *sanctification*) that gradually changes us from one thing into another. This is necessary because the ways of the world are so ingrained in our thinking and therefore our behaviour. Although God saves us immediately, instantly translating us out of death and into life, He does not instantly change the way we think and behave – that takes time! Over time our thinking will be corrected by a constant exposure to God's truth through His Word.

Joshua 1:8 and Romans 12:1-2 both confirm this:

"This book of the law shall not depart out of thy mouth; but thou shalt meditate therein day and night, that thou mayest observe to do according to all that is written therein: for then thou shalt make thy way prosperous, and then thou shalt have good success."

(JOSHUA 1:8)

"I beseech you therefore, brethren, by the mercies of God, that ye present your bodies a living sacrifice, holy, acceptable unto God, which is your reasonable service. And be not conformed to this world: but be ye transformed by the renewing of your mind, that ye may prove what is that good, and acceptable, and perfect, will of God."

(ROMANS 12:1-2)

What we believe in our heart and the way in which our thought patterns operate in our mind are absolutely pivotal in determining our self-worth. The mind is the place where thoughts are birthed that eventually establish themselves as beliefs, and our beliefs determine our actions in life. If we believe, for instance, that a particular need of ours will be met by going in a certain direction, then we will head in that direction. Whether it turns out to be right or not is another matter! But we will always act according to what we believe to be true.

The Bible is teaching us in these verses that *the way to a right life is right thinking.* Thinking that is aligned with the Word of God will result in godly beliefs, which will, in turn, result in godly actions and the affirmation of our Father which will increase our self-worth. This is the biblical antidote to a lack of self-worth and value. Many people can testify to the fact that their lives were truly changed only after they learned to think differently.

These verses also encourage us because God makes it plain to us that He wants us to succeed and be prosperous in life. It is His desire for us to work hard, have goals, be an example to others and succeed in life. Since the world takes so much notice of those who are prosperous, how amazing would it be if everything about our life could attract others and then point to the fact that it is God who has blessed us in this way? – that a simple obedience to His Word is the reason for our success!

When we are truly aligned with God's Word we really have something to offer those who do not know Jesus – true blessing and prosperity – not as the world knows it, which is fleeting and vague, but in an eternal, imperishable way.

> *"Weakness" in God's eyes is very valuable
> because it speaks of a person's ability to fully
> depend upon Him.*

Everything in God's Economy Has Value

In 1 Corinthians 1:27-29 Paul writes,

> *"But God hath chosen the foolish things of the world*
> *to confound the wise; and God hath chosen the weak*
> *things of the world to confound the things which are*
> *mighty; and base things of the world, and things which*
> *are despised, hath God chosen, yea, and things which*
> *are not, to bring to nought things that are: That no flesh*
> *should glory in his presence."*

If these verses tell us anything, it is that our Heavenly Father has a completely different set of criteria for judging people than we do! The key phrase that crops up several times here is "of the world". So when Paul says, "the foolish things *of the world*" he means people that are foolish in the world's eyes. God is not calling us "foolish" or "weak" or "base" or "despised" or saying we are of no consequence. That may be how the world regards us, but God sees something different.

What should encourage us greatly here is that God can use anyone, despite what they think of themselves and regardless of what others think of them. God's view of us is so radically different to the world's view! There is a complete reversal here of the world's values. The world thinks of weakness as a very negative trait. God calls it an asset! "Weakness" in God's eyes is very valuable because it speaks of a person's ability to fully depend upon Him. A weak person is a person who won't attempt to rely on their own ability. God's methods go completely against the world's methods and they are unfathomable to those who are not spiritually minded.

The Power of Encouragement

Our Father God is offering us a great deal of encouragement through the Scriptures we have looked at so far. We know that He is committed to our success and prosperity, and we also know that He wants to work through us regardless of how the world judges us, because He sees us very differently.

Encouragement is a powerful tool. People who have a very positive self-image can often trace it back to being encouraged a great deal by their parents and peers. The saying goes, "If you encourage someone for long enough, they just might begin to believe it!" There is a lot of truth in this. Have you noticed how often the smallest bit of encouragement delivered at the right time can make a big difference to someone? The odd thing about encouragement is – it's something that we all want (in fact as much as we can get hold of), yet it's the one thing we so often forget to offer to others!

Parents play a huge role in establishing their children's sense of self-worth through encouragement. Where people have never been encouraged in any shape or form, they often have an overwhelming sense of worthlessness until God takes hold of their life and heals them. But children who have been shown love, affection, affirmation and encouragement grow up very differently. We have a lot to learn from Americans in this regard. Anyone who has spent time around an American family will notice how frequently they affirm their children in public. Maybe we British are just too reserved! Our American cousins are not at all embarrassed to openly encourage and affirm. It is a part of their culture to do so. Maybe that's why there are so many American entrepreneurs. They have grown up in a "can do" culture that is constantly telling them, "Go for it. You *can* do it!"

Never mind what anyone else has said. What does God say about us? It's only His opinion that matters!

Truth or Lies?

We tend to go through life constantly making judgements about ourselves. We like to tell ourselves that we are reasonably intelligent and reasonably attractive. Maybe we tell ourselves that we know how to make others laugh and base much of our self-worth on that ability? We like to think that others accept us and enjoy our company.

So what robs us of our self-worth? When we can't tick all or any of those boxes! These things matter to us a great deal and so we find it difficult if we think we are not acceptable to others in some way. But one of the things we have to acknowledge is that some of these perceptions are based on reality and some of them are based on lies.

We may feel, for instance, that we are not particularly intelligent and as a result we feel inferior around others and lack self-worth. But what is that based on? How intelligent is "intelligent"? Is it possible to quantify exactly how much more intelligent we would like to be? No, it's not. So as long as we have enough intelligence to get by in life, what does it really matter? The fact is, Almighty God made us how we are and He is very happy with us. He accepts us completely, because He designed us. We only worry about how intelligent we are because somebody somewhere told us that it matters. Remember 1 Corinthians 1:27-29!

But perhaps our perception of our intelligence is founded on a lie, because of things that were spoken over us when we were younger? Maybe we were called "a late developer" or "non-academic" and we have worn those labels into adulthood. In which case, the problem is not our level of intelligence at all, but our wrong thought processes.

When I was at school I never read a book unless I was forced to. My mum refers to me now (though not in a negative sense) as a "late starter!" It used to take me a while to latch onto what the teachers were saying. After I gave my life to Jesus, however, I found myself wanting to read. I read books about people's testimonies and what God had done for them and the more I read, the more I had a hunger to read! Now I get huge enjoyment out of reading and studying – perhaps because God is at the heart of it!

My point is, what is said to us and what we believe as a result can make a huge difference to us, even though it may not be true. This is why it is so vital that we immerse ourselves in God's Word and absorb the truth. We need to know about everything that God is speaking over our lives. Never mind what anyone else has said. What does God say about us? It's only His opinion that matters!

SUMMARY

- Our self-worth is affected by the world's values and systems of attributing worth. We have also been affected by the influence of our parents, family and peers.

- The world's method of evaluation is only concerned with where we have come from and what we have achieved; whether we are successful or not according to its standards and whether our image is comparable to the world's "ideal".

- Those living outside of Jesus have been blinded spiritually, so their criteria for assessing worth is completely skewed and out of alignment with God's truth. We need to align ourselves with His Word in order to see our true worth.

- Our Father does not view us as others (or even we ourselves) view us. What the world calls weak, God wants to use. He is committed to our success and prosperity.

- Many of our perceptions about ourselves are founded on lies. We need to establish our lives upon the truth of God's Word. What He has to say about us is what really counts.

CHAPTER 2

THE ISSUE OF PRIDE

In the previous chapter we looked at the factors which are integral in shaping our self-worth and which inform our view and perception of who we are. We saw that one of the greatest of these "influences" is the world system we find ourselves in. In 1 John chapter 2, the Apostle John goes straight to heart of what this "world system" is all about and what effect it has on those who are immersed in it.

> *"Love not the world, neither the things that are in the world. If any man love the world, the love of the Father is not in him. For all that is in the world, the lust of the flesh, and the lust of the eyes, and the pride of life, is not of the Father, but is of the world. And the world passeth away, and the lust thereof: but he that doeth the will of God abideth for ever."*
>
> (1 JOHN 2:15-17)

John shows us that, as believers who love God, we need to be "shielded" from the effects of the world. He instructs us to do this by loving God and doing His will. As we continue to do this we are *in the world* but not *of the world*. The effects of being *of the world* i.e. immersed in and influenced by the world system, the Apostle lists as follows:

- The lust of the flesh
- The lust of the eyes
- The pride of life

These three are characteristic of the nature of the world and simply sum up the nature of and motivation behind man's sinfulness. In up-to-date language we might translate these three as,

- Sensuality, lust, immoral behaviour

- Materialism, greed, always striving for more

- Arrogance, ignorance of God, assurance in one's own resources and abilities

It is the last of these three – pride – that I want to focus on particularly in this chapter.

It might seem strange to some readers to discuss the issue of *pride* in a book about self-worth. But pride – an odd kind of *inverted pride* – is so often used by people to mask their insecurities. Webster's Dictionary defines the word "inverted" as, "to turn in a contrary direction, turn upside down, to change or reverse the order". This is what many people have done: they have been confronted by their own shortcomings or fears and have decided to obscure them from being seen by others by putting on a front.

Pride can be defined as an unreasonable conceit or taking a superior view of ourselves compared to others. We have all met people who have perhaps surprised us by their attitudes towards others and who it would be easy for us to simply label "arrogant" or "full of themselves". But we often see a pattern in such behaviour that indicates something deeper is happening under the surface:

- They are dismissive of others
- They frequently draw attention to other people's faults
- They are quick to criticize others
- They often talk about themselves or their achievements
- They despise weakness in others

All of these characteristics are telltale signs that a person is *masking* a void of self-worth inside. People who despise weakness in others are really despising those weaknesses in their own lives and running from them. People who are intolerant of other people's inadequacies usually feel inadequate themselves. Deep down they are uncertain about who they really are, what their value is, and where they fit into the world. I believe there are very few people in this world, if any, who don't suffer from some level of self-doubt. We are simply experts at covering it up! It is a camouflage for the true state of our beings.

We indulge in the art of negative comparison, looking for deficiencies in others or comparing ourselves unfavourably against their strengths. What the Bible is telling us to do is to esteem others – to respect and honour them, to bless their strengths. The enemy has so perverted the way in which we compare ourselves with others. It results in stemming the flow of mutual honour, respect, love and unity which should characterise the Body of Christ.

The Trap of Comparison

One of the things that people with inverted pride often do is to compare themselves with others. This results in thought patterns which dominate their thinking such as,

"I may be weak in this area, but I'm not as bad as that person ..."

"I'm definitely better looking than they are ..."

"Why can't I be like that person, they are so much more together than I am? ..."

"...when they measure themselves and compare themselves with one another, they are without understanding and behave unwisely."

(2 CORINITHIANS 10:12B)

Comparison is one of the biggest contributors to a lack of self-worth. It has two main effects:

It causes us to examine others and look for their weaknesses. With a kind of warped logic, we think that finding things to criticize in others will bolster our own self-esteem. It is the "I'm better than you" scenario.

It causes us to spend a great deal of time looking inward and examining ourselves, focusing only on our weaknesses. It is the "Everyone is better than me and I feel useless" scenario.

Both are equally dangerous places to be. In the first scenario we fall foul of judging others. We criticize and put people down when our Heavenly Father is calling us to encourage and build them up. In the second scenario we spend so much time putting ourselves down that we forget who we are "in Christ" – a valued, esteemed child of God with a specific purpose and calling – and the enemy manages to keep us bound up and ineffective in God's kingdom, because the truth is, no one rises above what they believe they are capable of.

The way out of both of these traps of comparison is to completely reverse them. The Bible takes a positive and completely opposite approach to building our self-esteem. God's method is to get us to focus on making favourable comparisons and this has an incredible healing effect on our own self-esteem.

What does this mean for us?

We turn comparison on its head and into something beautiful for Father God, our Creator, by beginning to admire the God-given gifts we see in others. Instead of focusing on and criticizing the negatives, we look for the positives and commend them. Instead of feeling threatened by someone else's gifting, we begin to celebrate it. It is so tempting, when we see someone doing something well, to think that we should be doing it too, or that we should be able to do it as well as they can. Stop comparing! Simply admire it.

One of the most healing and releasing things we can do in life is to look for and discover the gifts that are unique to us. When we see how God has made us and begin to enjoy and nurture the gifts He has invested in us, we stop worrying about what other people are doing or what they think of us, and life takes on a new richness. We also begin to appreciate it more when we see others operating in their gifts. It becomes so much easier to say, "I love the way you do that" or "you are very gifted in that area". It is personally liberating for us, and it is an added blessing to see how positively people react when you encourage them.

Paul addressed this issue in his letter to the Philippians:

"Fulfil ye my joy, that ye be likeminded, having the same love, being of one accord, of one mind. Let

31

nothing be done through strife or vainglory; but in lowliness of mind let each esteem other better than themselves. Look not every man on his own things, but every man also on the things of others. Let this mind be in you, which was also in Christ Jesus: who, being in the form of God, thought it not robbery to be equal with God: but made himself of no reputation, and took upon him the form of a servant, and was made in the likeness of men: and being found in fashion as a man, he humbled himself, and became obedient unto death, even the death of the cross. Wherefore God also hath highly exalted him, and given him a name which is above every name: that at the name of Jesus every knee should bow, of things in heaven, and things in earth, and things under the earth; and that every tongue should confess that Jesus Christ is Lord, to the glory of God the Father."

(PHILIPPIANS 2:2-11)

People with issues of low self-esteem generally think that other people are better than they are and, according to Paul, the advice of God's Word on this topic is: *go ahead and think that other people are better than you are.* Hang on – that doesn't sound right, does it?! It is right, but it is so different to what we are used to. We indulge in the art of negative comparison, looking for deficiencies in others or comparing ourselves unfavourably against their strengths. What the Bible is telling us to do is to *esteem others* – to respect and honour them, to bless their strengths. The enemy has so perverted the way in which we compare ourselves with others. It results in stemming the flow of mutual honour, respect, love and unity which should characterise the Body of Christ.

The biblical method of thinking of others as better than ourselves does not diminish our self-worth at all, it actually has the effect of building it up. We bless others and so God blesses us. In humility we apply God's Word by being obedient to His command and He fulfils His Word to us:

"For whosoever exalteth himself shall be abased; and he that humbleth himself shall be exalted."

(LUKE 14:11)

Preferring others and their needs before our own cultivates in us a servant heart which God honours and it has the effect of lifting our eyes off ourselves, our feelings of inadequacy, and our self-indulgent thoughts and desires. When we become outward-focused, rather than inward-focused, it transforms us! If we are constantly battling with worrying about ourselves and what people think of us, then the enemy has us tied up and there is no room in our hearts to think about giving out to others. This clever trick can seriously hinder the progress of our faith. The whole of the Christian life is about Jesus being given for us and us giving of ourselves to others because of Him. Paul says in these verses that Jesus "emptied Himself" and made Himself of "no reputation" for us. The Lord Jesus laid Himself as low as He possibly could in order to lift us up. Jesus, who was equal with God, deliberately brought Himself down to our level. When we begin to do the same for others we will be released from the negative comparison traps that hold us back in life.

Crucially, humility leads us to one amazing biblical truth, so important and so central to our walk with God that I can hardly overstate it. Humility teaches me that, I am nothing without Him!

Humility

The Bible has much to say about humility that we can learn from. The concept of humility has been hijacked by the world and had a different meaning applied to it, which is why many people struggle with the concept that we are to humble ourselves before others. The world defines humility in negative terms, such as:

- Being embarrassed
- Being made to feel worthless
- Not being good at anything
- Signifying a lack of self-assertion and drive

A stupid attitude, because everyone ought to push themselves forward.

Above all it sees humility as dangerous because it makes us vulnerable.

Biblical humility is, of course, very different and brings many rewards. Crucially, humility leads us to one amazing biblical truth, so important and so central to our walk with God that I can hardly overstate it. Humility teaches me that I am nothing without Him!

This does not mean we are worth nothing.
It does not mean we have no merit.

Instead it reveals the immeasurable truth that when we empty ourselves of all reliance on our own resources, when we lay our lives down in surrender to the Messiah on a daily basis, God's amazing power can begin to pour through our lives. The effect of this is that suddenly we have an immensely strong sense of our identity in Jesus and a strong sense of self-worth and purpose.

The world system elevates self-reliance and independence above all else. It hates the idea of a person making themselves vulnerable. How we have been robbed! How often we struggle against God because we have been polluted by the world's thinking, when we should be co-operating with Him and receiving His blessing.

Though humble people will often say and do things that the world finds strange (because it is so opposite to the world's way of thinking), they have an incredible sense of self-identity. They walk with a quiet spiritual authority and power because they know Almighty God's anointing on them. They know that whatever they accomplish for God, He supplied the power and ability that enabled them to do it. It seems backwards logic as far as the world is concerned, but *cultivating humility is a key to the door of self-worth.*

The great preacher, Charles Haddon Spurgeon, said that Jesus was the divine example of love and self-denial and urged us to copy His example. Let's stop worrying about what we can and can't do. Let's stop comparing ourselves to others and either being down on them or down on ourselves. Jesus made Himself of no reputation and we need to do the same, repenting of our pride and laying down our own abilities. Not to diminish our self-worth, but to truly find it in Christ. We are nothing without Him, but we are everything with Him!

SUMMARY

- The Apostle John highlighted for us the three issues that characterize the world's system and sum up all of man's sin: the lust of the flesh, the lust of the eyes and the pride of life. The last of these, pride, can often be a mask for an underlying lack of self-worth.

- Pride often sets out to attack in others what it is trying to disguise in the individual themselves, such as despising other's weaknesses or criticizing their faults. Very few people, if any, have no self-doubt that they are trying to hide.

- Comparing ourselves with others is a major contributor to a lack of self-worth and has two main effects:

  1. We think that pulling other people down will somehow lift us up.

  2. It causes us to become introverted and down on ourselves.

- The biblical escape route for these scenarios is unexpected and yet incredibly effective.

  1. We choose to esteem others above ourselves and by so doing, God takes responsibility for lifting us up.

  2. By practising humility God is able to pour His resources into our life.

- Humility is a key to a well balanced sense of identity and self-esteem but it unlocks the truth that "I am nothing without Him". This is the truth that brings true release and enables us to walk in God's power.

— *Prayers and Application* —

Take some time at the end of this section to reflect on the truths we have uncovered so far and apply them to your own life. Think in particular about how you view yourself and how you tend to think about yourself. Also consider how you believe God sees you, how you think others see you, and how you see others. Note down what you learn about yourself.

The remainder of this section contains a series of prayers for you to pray through. Not every single prayer will apply to you and your personal situation, but as you spend time in God's presence and allow the Holy Spirit to highlight certain issues in your life, use some of these set prayers to aid your conversation with God. Depending on what factors have contributed to a lack of self-worth in your life, it may be that you need the Father to bring healing and restoration. Open up to Him and invite the Holy Spirit to come and work in your life.

World's Values

"Father, first of all I want to repent of the ways in which I have co-operated with the world's values and allowed my mind to become polluted by its thinking. I no longer want to allow myself to be squeezed into its mould. Instead I want the truth of Your Word to shape my thinking, my attitudes and my actions. Amen."

Unhelpful Influences

"Father, I pray that You would break the power of any generational influences that have caused a pattern of

37

feelings of worthlessness to be established in me. I pray that You would break off any negative influences that have come via my parents, grandparents or from peers that have robbed me of self-esteem, and cleanse me from that in the name of Jesus. I thank You for the power of the blood of Jesus to break the negative cycles in my life and bring me to a place of freedom."

Listening to Lies

"Father God, I repent of believing the lies of inadequacy that the enemy would like me to continue believing. I thank You that regardless of my past upbringing, regardless of the things that have happened to me that have damaged my self-worth, You are the Great Restorer. I ask You to begin a process of healing in my life by the power of Your Holy Spirit. Thank you that you have broken me out of the mould of my past life and blessed me with a new life in Christ."

Changing My Thought Patterns

"Lord Jesus, I pray that You would renew my mind and transform me by the power of Your Word and break the power of every lie that I have believed regarding my self-worth. Break the power of the enemy's deception in my life and help me to see myself as You see me, Lord. Instead of always focusing on my weaknesses, help me to recognise the giftings that you have deposited in me and help me to focus on those strengths. I make a decision today to stop comparing myself to others and to acknowledge that You made me a unique person with unique qualities which You love. Give me a fresh revelation of Yourself today, Lord Jesus, so that You and not other people become the plumb-line and guidance for my life."

A Prayer to Forgive Anyone

Parents, grandparents, siblings, peers, work colleagues – anyone who has spoken negatively into your life, causing you to feel hurt or belittled, and who has damaged your self-worth:

"Father God, today I want to forgive those people who, past or present, have influenced my self-worth with their discouragement or disparaging words. Even though they chose to focus on the negative or to criticise, I choose to completely forgive them, Lord, and I no longer hold it against them. I pray that You would heal the damage that was done, Father God, and work with Your restoring power in my life."

Putting Myself Down

"Father God, I repent of the fact that, over the years, I have often criticised and spoken negatively about myself. Please forgive me. Today I declare that I accept who I am in You; I thank You that You made me and that You accept me fully. I lay down all my self-will and ask You to work in my life to transform it into something beautiful that brings glory to You. I surrender to Your plan for my life. Forgive me, Father, also for the fact that I have often co-operated with the enemy's lie that I am worthless. Thank You that I am incredibly valuable in Your sight and that, 'in Christ', my life has meaning and purpose."

"I am crucified with Christ: nevertheless I live; yet not I, but Christ liveth in me: and the life which I now live in the flesh I live by the faith of the Son of God, who loved me, and gave himself for me."

(GALATIANS 2:20)

CHAPTER 3

AREAS OF SELF-WORTH: PART 1

In the next two chapters we will take a closer look at the different areas in our lives that are affected by our self-worth. Some of these are *internal* because they are to do with our emotional and spiritual wellbeing and, as a result, are not immediately noticed by others. But some are *external*, such as how our self-image affects the way in which we dress or how we spend our money. At the end of this chapter I have included some scriptures to pray through as you seek to bring your self-worth into line with how your Father views you.

> God's message to us is a constant stream of, "You are precious to me ... your worth is immeasurable, that's why I sent My Son to die for you ... you have an important role to play ..."

Mental Self-Worth

The battle for self-worth begins in the mind. We find it very easy to think negative thoughts about ourselves or about others. We will often reason things through in our minds and arrive at a negative conclusion. It is as though "negativity" is our default setting as humans. Have you noticed that it is much easier to be negative and to drag people down to our level than it is to be positive and to lift people up? Negativity is the line of least resistance, the easier route to take.

Many people find it very hard to change the way they think once they have ingrained ways of thinking, but it is possible to radically transform the way we think by the application of God's Word. It is possible to conquer our own minds and to have victory and success over old, negative thought patterns.

Scripture acknowledges the fact that actions and behaviour are changed by first addressing a person's mind, and that it is exposure to the supernatural power of God's living Word that will change a person's thought patterns.

"And be not conformed to this world: but be ye transformed by the renewing of your mind, that ye may prove what is that good, and acceptable, and perfect, will of God."

(ROMANS 12:2)

If you are troubled by negative thoughts that keep your self-worth low, then the solution is to fill your mind with the truths of God's Word. The book of Romans in particular has a great deal to say about our position in Christ – what God has made us to be, who we are in Him, how He views us. The more you fill your mind with these truths, the more they will cancel out the lies of the enemy.

It sounds simple and obvious, but whatever you give the most thought-space to in your mind is what will shape your personality the most. We live in a world that bombards us constantly with messages and information, so it's often difficult to find some "head space" in which to order our thoughts. But this is why it's ever more vital that we set aside time in our life to be still before God and to read Scripture and dwell on its truth. There are no quick fixes in the Christian life, but if we constantly drip feed ourselves with God's Word, the effects are amazing.

In short, we need to give God a lot more access to our minds than the world or the enemy. The enemy's message to us is a constant stream of, "You're not worthy ... you're not important ... you're nothing ..." but God's message to us is a constant stream of, "You are precious to me ... your worth is immeasurable, that's why I sent My Son to die for you ... you have an important role to play ..."

We need to align ourselves with God's truth and stop listening to the lies.

In 2 Corinthians 10, Paul advises us what to do when ungodly thoughts come into our minds:

"Casting down imaginations, and every high thing that exalteth itself against the knowledge of God, and bringing into captivity every thought to the obedience of Christ ..."

(2 CORINTHIANS 10:5)

In other words, every thought that is contrary to the Word of God and what God wants for our lives, must be "taken captive" and handed over to Jesus. The sense of the original Greek words here is "taken by the spear", so when those negative thoughts come, we quickly "spear" them – we pin them down and refuse to let them live in our minds for more than a fleeting second.

The Bible teaches us that our minds can be so renewed that we have "the mind of Christ":

"For who hath known the mind of the Lord, that he may instruct him? but we have the mind of Christ."

(1 CORINTHIANS 2:16)

How do we have the mind of Christ? By filling our minds with the truth of the Word which leads to a deeper understanding of the heart of Father God and His will for us. It is not done nearly as much as it used to be when I was a young girl, but it is really helpful to try to memorise portions of Scripture. Then, when negative thoughts come to attack your self-worth, you can easily counter them with the truth. The more you meditate on the truth, the more the negative thought patterns in your mind will be erased.

> *What will build our self-worth is the input of positive, affirming encouragement, but we need to realise that the true affirmation we need comes only from God.*

Emotional Self-Worth

Our emotions and how we handle them play a large part in determining our self-worth. Often people talk about feeling "down" or "low" and this is usually due to a process something like this taking place inside them:

- They allow negative thoughts in their mind to go unchecked

- These negative thoughts become established as things they believe to be true about themselves

- Their emotions suffer as a result of believing these truths and concluding that they have less worth than others

- This can manifest itself in many ways: anxiety, depression, even anger

- The emotions begin to affect our actions and behaviour

Can you see how the mind/emotions can interact to create a dangerous downward spiral?

Some, because they have constantly listened to negative dialogue in their minds, can feel their emotions constantly being tossed backwards and forwards. They are very much affected by the words that others speak to them. They may, for instance, feel manipulated, pushed around and controlled by others, even when this is not necessarily the case. They may feel rejected by people, even when this is not true, because they have taught themselves to expect this. Others, because they feel emotionally vulnerable, will do the manipulating, pushing, controlling and rejecting themselves before anyone can do it to them. Other people go on the route of attention seeking to try to fill the emotional deficit they feel in their lives.

Often we feel that no one else can see, or is aware of, the state of our emotional wellbeing, but the fact is, it radiates out of us. As much as we think we are hiding our lack of self-worth, often it is plainly obvious to others by the way we speak, act and react emotionally to what life throws at us. You may have come across people who, when you offer them genuinely constructive criticism or advice, will take offence or feel crushed by your words. This behaviour is simply highlighting an issue in their soul that needs to be dealt with. By way of contrast, it is equally obvious to others when God has renewed and restored our soul – our countenance and the way in which we speak, act and react, is noticeably different.

The way in which we think about ourselves can cause an endless variety of emotional responses. Here are a few more examples:

- Some people constantly worry about others and their wellbeing because it takes the focus off themselves. It is easier to worry about others than to face their own emotional pain.

- Some find it very difficult to express their emotions and deal with the issues of their poor self-image because they fear that others will judge them.

- Some are not "happy" emotionally unless they are constantly being praised and anything negative said to them will cause them to react adversely. This reaction could be one of anger and defensiveness or it could be to go into a spiral of depression and self-recrimination.

- Some constantly boast about themselves/their achievements, not out of arrogance, but to try to elevate their self-image.

- Some are constantly trying to do things to "please" others because they believe it will result in them being liked and accepted and as a result their self-worth will increase.

Whatever the state of our emotions personally and whether we recognise ourselves in one of these examples or not, we all need to come to a place of balance. What will build our self-worth is the input of positive, affirming encouragement, but we need to realise that the true affirmation we need comes only from God. It's great when other people acknowledge and affirm us, but ultimately our emotional security must come directly from Him, otherwise we have no real security at all. When we develop a deep relationship with Father God, we can be sure that all our emotional needs will be fully met. For instance, if we feel the need to be accepted, we need to know that we are accepted by the Lord, because His Word tells us that we are loved by Him.

Don't be afraid to carry out some self-analysis here and allow the Holy Spirit to speak to you. The way in which we react to others is often very revealing. If, for instance, when people attempt to speak into your life, you tend to react fiercely or vigorously to defend your corner, that is not coming out of an emotionally-whole soul. This defensiveness is an indication that there is some emotional damage which needs to be healed. A balanced view would be that we don't always have to read things into what people are saying to us, thinking that they are criticising us or judging us harshly. A balanced view could take on board truly constructive criticism if we trust and respect the person, or if what they are saying rings true to us. If you find this difficult to deal with, then pray, "Lord, help me to rise above my feelings and help me to take out what is good and beneficial for me from what others say to me."

At the end of this section you will find some prayers to help you pray through these issues. When you come to that part, don't be afraid to cry and release your emotions. Crying is a way of releasing emotional pain, that releases stress from our bodies which could otherwise create very real physical problems. Sadly so many people deny themselves the right to cry. Don't be afraid to do it when you are in a safe place with God, working through these issues in prayer.

Learning to love ourselves
Those who feel a lack of self-worth can often find it difficult to accept that Jesus died for them. Perhaps they accept it in the general sense that they believe Jesus died for everyone, but they find it difficult to believe that if they were the only person on the planet, Jesus would still have died – *just for them.*

Do you think that if you were the only sinner alive on the planet, that Jesus would still have died for you?

Yes, He would! That is the message of the Gospel. It is so liberating to understand that God cares so personally for you, that He sent His Son to die on the cross just for you! That tells us just how much we are worth to Him.

Proverbs 19:8 says,

"He that getteth wisdom loveth his own soul; he that keepeth understanding shall find good."

This amazing verse tells us that if you want to nurture or "love" your own soul, then the way to do it is to immerse yourself in God's Word. I can't emphasise enough that the answer to our self-worth lies in the Bible and what God has to say about us. This is a great verse to remember when we are tempted to go off and explore other ways of fulfilling our emotional needs. Instead, we need to nurture our souls by meditating on God's Word, absorbing and "understanding" its truth so that our lives are changed. Understanding and applying God's Word is the path we need to walk in order to transform our self-image beyond recognition.

Physical Self-Worth

I am saddened that the spirit of the world is driving people from all walks of life to try to enhance their physical appearance. From cosmetic surgery to body piercings and markings, people are trying to gain acceptance by following fashion. This is a visual confirmation that people are being deceived that they are not good enough as they are.

Are they trying to compensate for a lack of inner self-worth which we will only find in the Saviour?

Almost without exception, the majority of people have an issue with some aspect of their body or physical appearance.

48

We are too tall, too short, too skinny, too fat; we don't like our nose, our ears stick out too much ... and the list goes on! Although our bodies are very important to us here on earth, the Bible promises that one day we will be given a heavenly body. At that point, all our worries about our bodies will be over, I'm sure. Until then, we have to put our earthly appearance into context.

We live in a society in the West where people are literally being ravaged by food disorders. It is deeply ironic that in the part of the globe where food is most readily available and affordable, so many people have so many problems with it. We overeat and obesity is a national epidemic. Others suffer from anorexia or bulimia. The Western "body image" portrayed through fashion on TV or in magazines showing "size zero" models has much to answer for in making people paranoid about their bodies.

Yet, God loves and cherishes each one of us. He formed us and made us, and He loves us perfectly. God loves the way you and I look! Otherwise He would have designed us differently. God takes notice of people's physical appearance because Scripture takes the time to describe its different characters to us. Leah was "tender eyed" ... Rachel was "beautiful" ... David had a "ruddy" complexion.

Isaiah 53 gives us an intriguing description of Jesus:

"For he shall grow up before him as a tender plant, and as a root out of a dry ground: he hath no form nor comeliness; and when we shall see him, there is no beauty that we should desire him."

(ISAIAH 53:2)

When I read this verse recently, it struck me that it seems Jesus was not an outstandingly good looking man. This tells me that outward appearance is far less important to God than it is to us. Someone who is outstandingly beautiful on the inside has far more to offer people than someone who is gorgeous or handsome on the outside. Perhaps God didn't want people to be distracted by His good looks when Jesus walked into a room. I suspect He wanted Jesus' inner beauty to be the thing that attracted others to Him. When beauty comes from within – that's when it's real!

God loves us, He made us, He likes the way we look, but it's not a high priority for Him. He is more concerned with the state of our heart and, in due course, we will be given a heavenly body that will far surpass our earthly form. We need to keep these things in perspective when we are tempted to grumble about how we look.

But neither should we neglect our bodies. Whether we are happy with the size and shape of our bodies or not, we have a responsibility in this area of our wellbeing. There is a balance we must maintain in order to keep our bodies healthy and functioning correctly which includes our patterns of rest, exercise and our eating habits. In a world that heavily promotes eating for pleasure, we need to remember that, actually, we eat for nourishment and strength. Sometimes we can be our own worst enemy in the area of our physical wellbeing, simply because we don't look after ourselves properly.

> *Self-hate or self-loathing is a lie of the enemy.*
> *It is a deliberate tactic designed to keep us*
> *from realising who and whose we are.*

Self-Worth In Our Soul

Our soul is the part of us that contains our personality, our will, our intellect, our "heart" or emotions – everything that makes up the "invisible" person. Ask yourself this question: *"Do I know who I am?"*

It's the one challenging question that people are constantly grappling with. Some people will drift through life and never really find out who they are. Others will look for things to give them their sense of identity – their work, their relationships or a particular cause are all common "solutions". But what happens when those things are taken away?

Some people get married and lose their identity in that of their partner, but one day, if they find themselves widowed or divorced, they are left asking themselves, "Who am I now?" What about the man who draws all his self-worth from his important and high-powered job, but then finds himself made redundant and unable to get work? What happens to the feelings of wellbeing in his soul then?

We all need to be secure in our sense of identity, because it feeds our soul. We feel at peace and secure in the knowledge of who we are. But that sense of wellbeing can only come from realising our identity in God's Son. It cannot be reliant on the many temporal things in this life. Otherwise, before long we will be robbed of our identity.

Maybe you have not invested your soul into temporal things, and yet you still feel a sense of isolation? Do you feel alone in a crowd? Do you feel less worthy and important than others much of the time? Do you worry about whether people accept you? God can minister to you in this area and He can bring healing and wholeness into your soul. If this describes how you feel, there are some prayers you can pray through at the end of this section.

Some people experience problems feeling at peace in their soul because they don't allow themselves to express their true personality. Their "personality" is one that they have created that they believe is acceptable to themselves and to others. It's not their true personality, but a carefully constructed façade. Part of coming to Jesus involves the submission of our will to His will. As we do this, He is able to minister to us, transforming us by the power of the Holy Spirit, and increasingly He enables us to "become" or "be ourselves".

Problems occur when we don't want to let go of the persona we have created for ourselves. It makes us reluctant to surrender our will to Christ's will because we think we will have to change. That is true – we will! But Jesus loves us completely and His only desire is to release us to truly be ourselves. Many people experience a breakthrough in their soul/emotions when they are prepared to say, "Father, I submit my will to Your will. I want the best You have for me. I want what You want." This releases our Heavenly Father to begin a process of healing and transformation in us.

Linked to this issue, another common problem people fall into is that of hating themselves. Self-loathing is the opposite of self-worth. How can anyone enjoy feelings of security rooted in their self-worth if they are working against themselves? It's impossible. Self-hate or self-loathing is a lie of the enemy. It is a deliberate tactic designed to keep us from realising who and *whose* we are. The antidote to self-hate is to understand who we are in Christ. When we understand how valuable and precious we are to God, it changes our view of ourselves. We need to realise that we are loved children of our Father and joint-heirs with Christ (see Romans 8:17). We are accepted and beloved in God's family.

Take some time to dwell on and pray through the following Scriptures. There are literally dozens of references in the Bible that tell you how your Father feels about you – truths that express your position, right now, in Christ. Here is just a sample. We will return to these truths again and expand on them in the final chapter.

In Jesus, God's Son, you are ...

- A child of God (Romans 8:16)
- Justified (Romans 5:1)
- Forgiven (Colossians 1:13-14)
- A new creation (2 Corinthians 5:17)
- Redeemed from the enemy (Psalm 107:2)
- Delivered from the power of darkness (Colossians 1:13)
- Sanctified (1 Corinthians 6:11)
- Kept in safety wherever you go (Psalm 91:11)
- Saved by grace through faith (Ephesians 2:8)
- An inheritor of eternal life (1 John 5:11-12)

Summary

- The battle for our self-worth begins in our mind. We find it easier to be negative about things than positive and we frequently find it hard to change the way we think. This is why it is vital that we fill our thinking with the truth of God's Word. The Bible has the ability to renew our mind and this is what starts the process of transformation in us, as Romans 12:2 explains.

- Our emotions play a large part in determining our self-worth. We need to realise that our emotions are constantly "fuelled" by our thought life. If we constantly allow negative thoughts to dominate our mind, then our emotional wellbeing will suffer. By contrast, if we reinforce our thinking with positive thoughts and truths about who we are in Christ, we will grow in our emotional wellbeing.

- We need to come to a place of balance in our emotions, realising that true affirmation comes only from God. We appreciate it when other people affirm us, but we cannot establish our emotional security on this. Our security comes from God, or we have no real security.

- We live in a culture obsessed with image, but we should not let this dictate our self-worth. We need to understand that God loves and cherishes us. He loves what He made when He made you, so be careful about being self-critical concerning your image.

- Our sense of identity is important, because this feeds the soul. But our sense of identity, and the wellbeing it imparts, can only come from realising and living in our identity in Jesus Christ. We need to be "real" with ourselves and others and avoid projecting an identity which is false, or that we believe others want to see in us. When we see how precious and valuable we are to God, this greatly changes our perspective on who we are.

CHAPTER 4

AREAS OF SELF-WORTH: PART 2

Self-Worth and Our Appearance

These days I very rarely have cause to visit the local branch of my bank, but recently I needed to go there to sort something out. I admit, I hadn't been into a high street bank for a long time, and by saying what I'm about to, I run the risk of sounding terribly old-fashioned – but I was shocked by the appearance of the bank staff! Years ago, my bank was populated by smartly dressed people in suits who looked ready to do business, so I was surprised to find myself being served by a girl in tight jeans with a bare midriff whose hair was at least seven different colours! Whilst I was in the bank, I noticed another girl wearing an outrageous dress that looked more suited to a nightclub than an office.

Why was all this bothering me? You may ask. My problem was that the appearance of the staff undermined my confidence in the bank. "Do these people know what they're doing?" I wondered to myself. "Do they care about doing a good job?"

Whether we like it or not, our appearance says something about us. It tells others a lot about the type of person we are and what our values are. Now, what I didn't know was that the bank had "dress down" days, but this particular day was also a charity fund raising day, and they had pulled out all the stops to look outrageous! But, since I didn't know this, the way these girls were dressed spoke volumes to me about how they would treat me as a customer; i.e. casual dress = casual service!

My feelings got the better of me and eventually I spoke about it to the girl who was dealing with me.

"I cannot believe how people are dressed in here today!" I said.

"Is it a problem to you?" she asked.

"Well, it is actually, yes." I told her. "It looks very casual in here, but you're supposed to be looking after my money!"

"It's dress-down day," she informed me. "Why would it matter to you so much?"

"Because," I explained, "your dress code tells people a lot about you and this doesn't impress me much."

Call me cynical but was I surprised when two weeks later I received all the wrong paperwork in the post? No!

Our outward appearance communicates a strong message about what is going on inside us. Years ago I knew a young man called John who belonged to the youth group of my church. He was a very troubled individual and had a lot of personal issues. Once he came round to visit me and he stunk like a polecat! I asked him what he was doing and couldn't help but comment that it seemed like he hadn't washed in a week. "I haven't," he admitted, "now that I think about it." It shocked me that John was so caught up with the trauma and anguish inside him that he didn't even realise he hadn't washed. But this is how our internal wellbeing can affect our external appearance. Very often, when a person changes on the inside, they make an effort to change their outward appearance as well.

Our appearance has a strong bearing on how other people respond to us. How we appear to others goes a long way to determining how they react to us, whether they listen to us or not, whether they notice us or take us seriously. I find the following questions challenging to ask ourselves when thinking about our appearance:

• Am I aware of the way in which I present myself to others?

• What does my appearance say about what is going on inside me?

Some people tend to dress down and wear muted coloured clothing because they want to blend into the background and not stand out. Because of a lack of self-worth they shy away from drawing attention to themselves. But it can work the opposite way around too. Others wear bright clothes or daring clothes because of their lack of self-worth. Inside they are crying out to be noticed and they want to grab people's attention. Because of each individual's complex actions and reactions, it can be difficult to "read" people at times and to get to the heart of what they are all about. But we must get to the heart of it for ourselves. As Christians we want to radiate the presence of Jesus. We are ambassadors of the Lord Jesus!

One of my personal hobby horses is that men should look like men and women should look like women. I think it's important for us to bear this in mind and understand its importance in a world that is trying to blur the boundaries between the genders. Today there are women who dress like men and men who dress like women! Sometimes it seems as though society is trying to drive us towards becoming unisex people. We need to preserve the uniqueness of the genders God created and celebrate our individuality.

As believers, we all need to consider how we manage our appearance. Because how we look communicates so much to others, we want our appearance to be honouring to Father God – to communicate something of Him to others. We don't have to mindlessly follow fashion, but we can create our own unique style. Jesus made us unique, so let's be unique.

1 Timothy 2:9 (Amplified Bible) says,

> *"Also [I desire] that women should adorn themselves modestly* and *appropriately and sensibly in seemly apparel, not with [elaborate] hair arrangement or gold or pearls or expensive clothing."*

This verse says something about the holiness, purity and simplicity with which we are to approach managing our appearance. It doesn't mean, ladies, that we shouldn't be wearing jewellery or doing wild things with our hair! Paul's point in writing was entirely different: the quality of our soul should be the first thing that people notice about us, not our appearance. Our inner person should be more beautiful than our outer person. As Isaiah 61:10 says,

> *"I will greatly rejoice in the Lord, my soul shall be joyful in my God; for he hath clothed me with the garments of salvation, he hath covered me with the robe of righteousness, as a bridegroom decketh himself with ornaments, and as a bride adorneth herself with her jewels."*

Years ago a young woman came to me on a prayer line. She was dressed in black and wearing very dark, heavy eye-liner. Chains were hanging from the pockets of her jeans and I saw the "spiritual chains" in her eyes as she came sobbing into my arms.

"I want Jesus to give me back my purity," she said soulfully, fingering an engagement ring. Her whole countenance said, "I have no self-worth and no confidence at all concerning my future marriage." I explained it was time to dress as a daughter of *the* King and to wear "robes of righteousness" as a pure, godly woman.

Her past was reflected in the pools of tears and I had the honour of imparting, in a few minutes, words that would put her on the right road of expressing herself and feeling priceless for both her Heavenly Father and her fiancé. Once I had prayed for her to be set free from worthlessness I encouraged her to wear flattering clothes and to get rid of the tight and over-revealing garments that only expressed her pain, not her soul, personality and self-worth.

I said, "Dress for your King and fiancé and make them both proud and 'walk in' the fact that Jesus has cleansed you and freed you from guilt and shame. The past has gone. HE HAS MADE YOU NEW!"

The next night a very different young woman attended the meeting. The black clothes of grief, the eye-liner which subconsciously said "keep away" were gone. She was beautifully turned out, colourful and she glowed as a soul only can when Jesus has sent away the stone-throwers. When the soul is freed from guilt and a feeling of unworthiness, and one receives a cleansing of the blood of Jesus, it shows in our appearance. She had now covered those parts that will be sacred to her and her husband and for them only in their future. Our eyes met and we both smiled and knew the power of His atoning blood. She shared that she was so relieved to have had the advice of an older woman, because she had no one else who would speak into her life in such a way.

Practical Self-Worth

Sometimes we can be faced with very practical issues in life and how good or bad we are at dealing with them can have a significant effect on our self-worth. How we are affected by this depends a great deal on context and circumstances. For example, someone who is dyslexic might find themselves in a church home group when someone passes them the Bible and asks them to read aloud from it. Being unwittingly thrust into a situation like this could really batter someone's self-confidence. Another example could be the person who has absolutely no sense of direction, who finds themselves lost in the middle of a strange town. Such a situation would really undermine their self-confidence.

Each of us has things we are good at and things we are not good at. That's the reality of life! But sometimes we feel, perhaps because of peer pressure or because of circumstances, that we have to be good at everything.

When it comes to practical things, I admit I am hopeless. I am the least practically-minded person I know. Fortunately, I have some good friends who are highly practical who turn up on my doorstep and get me out of trouble! I wouldn't know where to start with a hammer, chisel, or a needle and thread, but frankly, I don't want to! I can accept the fact that God has made me differently and my gifts lie in other areas.

We need to come to a place where we accept that there are some things we are good at and others we are not good at. Some people shy away from attempting things unless they think they can be really good at them. It's a defence mechanism designed to protect their self-worth from being dented. We shouldn't let such an attitude rob us of our self-worth! If we have to call in a plumber or some other skilled person to do a job for us, so what? Why should that affect us? Knowing our limitations as well as our abilities is a liberating thing. We don't have to be good at everything, so there is no point trying to be. We just need to be happy with who we are and what we can do.

When we are faced with things that we don't know how to handle, God wants to help us!

Expectation is an important factor when considering issues of self-worth. Some people have told me that they were brought up to be a "strong" or "capable" person. That meant they were expected to be able to do a lot of things for themselves and to be good at many things. But since no one can be good at everything, when they failed to perform well in certain areas, it knocked their confidence a great deal. A lack of ability in certain things even made them feel guilty. They thought, "I should be doing this myself, but I can't do it!" Many people suffer unnecessarily from this kind of pressure, particularly due to other people's expectations. Instead we need to show ourselves some grace and accept ourselves as our Heavenly Father accepts us. We can find our level and be happy with our abilities.

In life we often get into patterns of behaviour and create ruts for ourselves that we follow without thinking. After a while, we don't even realise what we are doing or why we are doing it! We do this just as much in the area of our self-worth. Some people defer to the opinions of others frequently because they want to be accepted and they see agreeing with others as a method of gaining acceptance. Others are reticent to share their thoughts with anyone in case someone "sees through" them and thinks they are stupid. Others will cover up any insecurity they feel by being brash and opinionated when dealing with other people. All these stereotypes and more have a bearing on our approach to practical issues. We need to examine our habits and then ask the Lord to give us wisdom and confidence in ourselves. Where we have been discouraged and had our confidence knocked, God wants to heal us.

Paul reminds us in Philippians 4:13,

"I can do all things through Christ which strengtheneth me."

It is a simple truth, but one we need to learn and apply to so many areas of our lives. When we are faced with things that we don't know how to handle, God wants to help us! If we ask for His help, time and time again God will give us the wisdom we need to unlock seemingly difficult circumstances or tasks.

Social Self-Worth

Each of us needs to reach a place where we are confident in ourselves and can take our rightful place in society. Self-confidence, especially in social settings, is important if we are going to interact with others on a meaningful level. We are all different in this respect. Some people are much more comfortable communicating with others on a one-to-one basis and they may feel awkward in a group setting. So, whenever they find themselves in a social group, they tend to be the quiet one and don't often share their thoughts. Others are much more comfortable communicating to groups of people. They like to be around others and maybe even being the centre of attention, freely speaking out and saying what they think. By contrast, these people may find it more difficult to communicate intimately on a one-to-one basis!

Whatever our natural disposition is, we all have to find our self-worth in God in order to mix with others successfully. When we are truly comfortable with who we are and who Father God made us to be, we will be much more successful in our communication and interaction with others. It's easy

64

to spot in any social group those people whose identity is rooted in things other than Jesus.

Some people spend a lot of time boasting about how good they are or what they have achieved in the past. Are they just arrogant? Or is there a deeper cause for this behaviour? Boasting tends to be a cover up and the people who do it are trying to justify their place in a social group. They are trying to convince others that they are successful and deserve to be liked and admired. They are sending out a signal that says, "Here is someone worth spending time with."

People who feel a general lack of acceptance will often try to "sell" themselves to others. This might manifest itself in various ways. There is the person who will spontaneously buy presents for others, not because of any special occasion or even simply because they love them, but in order to gain acceptance. There is nothing wrong with buying presents for people, of course, but it is good to question our motives for doing things – to ask ourselves, "Am I doing this just to bless this person or am I doing it because I crave their acceptance?"

Then there is the person who will talk incessantly in a group of people. In their mind they have formed an equation something like this: if people listen to me, then they must value me and if they value me then I will feel accepted. So, their solution is to talk constantly, almost "holding court" in their social group, in an effort to get people listening to them. What is particularly sad in this case is that this kind of social awkwardness will eventually drive people away and others may avoid inviting this person into social settings because of their habit of "taking people hostage".

We can learn from other people, without trying to be like them, just by seeing how they interact.

Other people will gather information on particular subjects in order to project themselves as an "expert" in a particular field or subject. Again, this is a method of gaining affirmation and acceptance. They feel that if they are really knowledgeable on a particular topic, then people will admire them and want to spend time around them. They try to flex their knowledge and intellectual muscle in order to impress others. Again, this can have a negative rather than a positive effect in social settings. People may avoid us, thinking, "Oh no, here he comes again. I'm going to get another lecture on software development ... rugby ... motor racing ..." or whatever our topic may be.

Another group of people will frequently talk about their problems in social settings and can alienate others by coming across as very "needy". All of us have needs, of course, but there are certain settings in which we can speak about our needs to those in a position to help, and certain settings where it is entirely inappropriate. Sharing our feelings in an unchecked manner in the latter setting can earn us a bad reputation and cause people to want to avoid us. We need to ask God for wisdom in social settings, so that we know the right time to speak up and the right time to remain quiet. If we find it difficult to judge how to behave or relate in social situations, it is a good idea to stand back and have a good look at what is going on. We can learn from other people, without trying to be like them, just by seeing how they interact.

If our self-worth is rooted in Jesus Christ, then we will display Christ-like behaviour in our social settings. As with every aspect of life, there is a time to give and a time to receive. We need to achieve that balance in social settings – to know how to give to people and how to receive from them. Ask yourself the following questions:

- Am I sensitive to the needs of others in my communication, or am I often oblivious? Am I always ready to listen to what others are saying, or am I too eager to jump in and say what I want to say?
- Am I ready to help others when I see their needs?
- Do I bring others encouragement?
- Do I make others feel valued and needed in social settings? How could I do this more?

Jesus wants to bless us and make us feel valued and welcome in His presence. We need to stand back and look at how we deal with other people, make sure that we are doing the same as Jesus, and remember that our worth comes from Him. As Paul writes in 2 Corinthians 3:5,

"Not that we are sufficient of ourselves to think anything as of ourselves; but our sufficiency is of God."

I recall a young man called Steve who used to speak very loudly and although he was not really confident when conversing, he used to wade into situations that he knew nothing about and speak as though he was an expert in this particular field! He would boast and try to articulate words to convince others HE WAS THE MAN WHO COULD SORT IT FOR THEM! As a result, people would get very irritated and be dismissive of him. He used to get into a lot of scrapes. I could see it was a cry for help and acceptance, and all he was trying to do was find his place in society to belong. Sadly, the false pride camouflaging all his inadequacies was so great that one could never get near to help him. This charade had been well practiced from childhood and the grooves of this walk were deep. Only the Lord could have got through to him and reach him where I had tried and failed. May we all keep our hearts open to the input of others. When they see our pain they want to help us. Let us be transparent before the Lord so that we get victory in our lives.

If we cannot receive for ourselves – whether it comes in the form of gifts, compliments, encouragement or help – then we have a problem.

Financial Self-Worth

Our self-worth has a direct impact on our finances – how we use and view money. We can all think of at least one person who thinks that money spent on them is a complete waste. Consciously or sub-consciously they have arrived at the conclusion that others are more worthwhile than they are, and therefore deserve to have money spent on them much more than they do on themselves. Often, those who manifest a difficulty in receiving from others have a self-worth deficit.

On the face of it, it appears a good thing – even a godly thing – to put others before ourselves. There is nothing wrong with being humble and preferring others before ourselves. But if we cannot receive for ourselves – whether it comes in the form of gifts, compliments, encouragement or help – then we have a problem.

The favourite sayings of people in this situation are things like, "Don't waste your money on me," or "I'll make do with what I've got," or "I wish what you're saying about me was true," or "Keep your money for something really important". It is important to have balance in life. There is no sense, for instance, in someone buying us extravagant gifts all the time that are well beyond their budget. In such an instance, we may well be justified in saying, "Don't waste your money!"

But neither should we deny others the pleasure of blessing us in ways that are appropriate. We should enjoy this, not feel guilty about it!

If we never treat ourselves or allow others to, it may be because we have an underlying fear of lack. Many people are fearful of going without or of not having enough. This can cause them to hoard things and to be very careful with their money – to the point where they go over the top and never allow themselves any luxuries. This is an area where we need to allow Jesus to come and help us because our attitude is out of balance. It's right that we should be good stewards of our resources, but again we have to examine our motives. Ask yourself:

• Do I derive much of my security from money?

• Do I fear going without or not having enough?

• Do I suffer from a poverty mentality?

We understand from Scripture that God is anything but stingy. On the contrary, He is amazingly generous and His heart is always to lavish His blessing upon us. Jesus taught us that as our Father, God takes responsibility for providing for His children's needs. Those who trust in Him will never go without. When we depend upon God for all our needs and put our faith in Him, He is delighted to step in and meet them.

If you feel you have suffered from a poverty mentality, then maybe it's time to break out of that mould. Begin by treating yourself to something – it could be the smallest thing – something that you wouldn't normally buy. Also, allow others to spend money on you and don't tell them off for doing it. You will find that this simple step can break something open for you spiritually. Allow God to minister to you and realise that you are of immense worth to Him.

Our Father's heart is always that we should bless and be blessed. If you feel that you are more than willing to receive from others, but they don't seem to give you anything, then begin by being a blessing to them. We shouldn't give in order to get, because that is a form of spiritual blackmail! But if we give to others with pure motives, genuinely desiring to bless them, God sees this and begins to store up blessing for us. As we continue to give out to others, God will begin to bless us, often in surprising ways from unexpected sources. The blessing may not come directly from those whom we've blessed, but God will ensure that we receive in ways that surpass that which we've given.

2 Corinthians 9:6-7 says,

"But this I say, he which soweth sparingly shall reap also sparingly; and he which soweth bountifully shall reap also bountifully. Every man according as he purposeth in his heart, so let him give; not grudgingly, or of necessity: for God loveth a cheerful giver."

Here we see the principle of sowing and reaping clearly illustrated. If we hold back from giving to others, then we will reap "sparingly". We will reap *something* back, but it may only just cover our basic needs. On the other hand, if we give generously and "cheerfully" (meaning liberally and without thought of reward) then we will reap amazing generosity in return. This is the virtuous cycle God has ordained.

Spiritual Self-Worth

In addition to finding our self-worth in all of the above areas, crucially we need to realise and nurture our spiritual self-worth. We need to understand and appreciate our place in the

Body of Christ, to know where we fit in and what we bring that is of value and worth.

In the Church there seems to be a self-worth phenomenon that expresses itself in one of two ways. There are those people who think that everyone else is better than they are – more valuable, more gifted, more accepted etc. Then there are those who are inflated with their own egos and think that they are more valuable, more gifted, more accepted! Obviously neither of these extremes is correct. But these games that we play make us an inwardly-focused, self-analytical community consumed with its own problems. In short, it means that people are not hearing the Gospel while we are caught up with our identity crises. Let's stop looking inwards and worrying about what the person next to us is doing and begin to look at what God wants us to accomplish.

Ask yourself,

- *What has God gifted me to do?* (God has given you a unique set of gifts and abilities. If you are unsure what you should be doing in the Body of Christ look first at your gifts).

- *What am I passionate about?* (Often, the things we are passionate about, when coupled with our God-given gifting tell us a lot about our place in the Body of Christ and point to what we should be doing).

- *How can I use my gifts to bless others in the Church?* (When God gives us gifts they are never just for ourselves, but for the benefit of the wider Body. God's gifts always have a corporate expression).

- *How can I use my gifts to bless others outside the Church?* (God's gifts also have an external expression. When we use our practical gifts and spiritual knowledge to bless people in the street, we make God's heart glad.

God has given us all spiritual gifts and we should be using them. Often people sit on their abilities and as a consequence miss out on so much. I once prayed for a lady during a ministry time who told me that fifteen years ago someone had prophesied over her. The gist of the prophecy was that God would open a door for her to pray with others in a special way and that He would move powerfully through her prayers. But, she had not acted on this word – instead she had been waiting for something to happen.

I asked her, "So you've been waiting for fifteen years?"

"Yes," she replied.

"What a shame," I said to her, "because the door is already open. We have been given a commission by Jesus to go out and minister to others. You need to stop waiting for an opportunity to fall into your lap and go out and get on with it!"

Tragically, this lady had been waiting for someone in her church to single her out and say, "We want *you* to come and pray for people." Because they had never done this, she was still waiting, still wondering about what God had said. If you are waiting for a door to open for you, just throw off your super-spiritual attitude and start walking!

We shouldn't allow our lives to be governed by prophetic words, because the Word of God is our ultimate guide and the plumb-line by which we measure our life – the Bible is very clear about what we should be doing. Jesus gave us clear directions to go out and minister to others, reaching out to the lost, hurting and broken with the love of Jesus. We don't need anyone to release us to do this – God has given us the permission to do it and the authority to do it with.

These things should be as natural to us as breathing, eating and sleeping. Everyone in the Body of Christ has worth and value and we all need each other to function properly. Look at the amazing picture that Paul shows us in 1 Corinthians 12:

"For the body is not one member, but many. If the foot shall say, Because I am not the hand, I am not of the body; is it therefore not of the body? And if the ear shall say, Because I am not the eye, I am not of the body; is it therefore not of the body?"

(1 CORINTHIANS 12:14-16)

We need to look at these verses afresh and realise again that we are a vital part of the Body of Christ. Everyone has a place and a function and interdependence within the Body. We are accepted and in turn we accept each other. In 2 Thessalonians Paul points to the reason why:

"Wherefore also we pray always for you, that our God would count you worthy of this calling, and fulfil all the good pleasure of his goodness, and the work of faith with power: That the name of our Lord Jesus Christ may be glorified in you, and ye in him, according to the grace of our God and the Lord Jesus Christ."

(2 THESSALONIANS 1:11-12)

The ultimate aim of us finding our place in the Body and using our gifts for God is to bring Jesus glory. As we find and accept our self-worth in Him and begin to live out our calling, it brings Jesus honour and His grace and power continues to work in our life. To honour Jesus and live by His grace – this is the ultimate expression of spiritual self-worth.

SUMMARY

- Our outward appearance can speak volumes about the state of our self-worth. It has an important bearing on how others respond and react to us. Whilst we do not want to become obsessive with image, our appearance should be honouring to God and communicate something of Father God to others.

- Some of us suffer a dent in our self-worth because we are not very practically minded. But then many people who are very practical are not necessarily creative, and *vice versa*. It doesn't matter which type of person you are, just that you come to a place of acceptance and peace about how God made you. God accepts us and loves us just as we are, so we need to learn to do the same.

- Expectations can be a trap in this regard. E.g. your father was very practical, so your family expect you to be practical as well. Or, one of your siblings is musically talented and your parents expect you to be, but you're not. These unmet expectations can produce guilt in us or feelings of insecurity. Again, the key is learning to become comfortable with the gifts God has given you.

- Whether we are naturally shy or outgoing, we can learn to socialise with others and "fit in" to social groups when we are comfortable with who God made us to be. Don't get caught up with comparing yourself to others. God made you to be unique! Remember that trying to "sell" yourself to others in order to get them to like you is nearly always counter-productive. People will either accept you for who you are or they won't. There is nothing we can do about this. Instead, we trust God to bring around us those who truly love and accept us and celebrate who we are.

- Finance is another area that can be revealing regarding our self-worth. We need to take a balanced approach here, which is to be content with all God has given us without striving for more, and to be able to accept gifts from others without guilt.

- Crucially, we must come to understand our spiritual worth before God. This is what helps us to find our place within the Body of Christ as we understand where we belong and what we bring that is of worth. Ask yourself what God has gifted you to do and how you can use your gifts to bless others.

— *Prayers and Application* —

At the end of this section, as in my previous book, I have included a number of set prayers to help people pray through some of the issues we have touched upon. Not every issue will be applicable to you, but allow yourself to open up to the Holy Spirit and ask Him to highlight the areas in your life that need attention.

Don't worry about making yourself vulnerable before God. Remember that He is not trying to catch you out or waiting to hit you with a big stick! Instead, as you humble yourself and bring certain issues before Him, He is willing to minister to you – to forgive you where there has been sin and to bring healing where there has been hurt.

Start by praying this prayer:

"Thank You, Father, that my self-worth is something that matters greatly to You. I pray that as I open my heart to You, You would minister Your peace to me – that I would rest from striving and trying to be someone I'm not and accept that You accept me as I am. Thank You that Jesus died for me in order to make me whole. You want me to be whole so that I can touch the lives of others, that the light of Christ might shine out of my life and be an example for others. Please change my heart and change my thinking as You need to. Help me to lay down the things in my life that don't really matter and to focus on the things that really do matter. Amen."

A Word of Knowledge

To some readers, I believe God is saying that you have felt "invisible" for a long time, like your life doesn't matter very much to anyone. Father God wants you to know that you matter very much to Him and He is calling you to step "out of the shadows" that you have occupied for so long, because He has a unique plan and purpose for your life. Pray the following prayer:

Coming Out of the Shadows

"Lord Jesus, You know that for a long time I have felt like I've been living in the shadows, obscured from view by other people. Thank You that Your desire for me is to come into the light and live in the fullness of self-worth that is mine in You. Thank You that I don't need to try to be like anyone else, because You value me just as I am and You are pleased with the way You made me. Today I can be myself with You. I don't need to hide any more. Today I make a choice to step out of the shadows and into the fullness of all that You have for me. Please guide me by Your Holy Spirit as I move forward with You. Thank You, Father God."

Our self-image will improve dramatically as we focus on the truth that God loves us perfectly as we are.

God wants to assure you of your identity in Jesus. Talk to Him about the issues that you know need dealing with in your life. Pray the following prayer if you feel you need to repent of going your own way and trying to find self-worth through your own efforts:

Seeking Self-Worth on the Wrong Path

"Father God, I'm sorry for the times when I have ignored You and tried to find my self-worth through various means instead of coming to You and asking You to meet my needs. I repent of trying to find my identity through relationships, through my work, even through my gifts. Forgive me. I come to You and ask You to fulfil my need for self-worth as only You can."

Wrong Attitudes of Heart

"Father, forgive me for the things that I have done and the choices I have made that have prevented me from living in the fullness of Your purposes for me. I repent of allowing myself to be sidetracked by issues such as holding onto unforgiveness, bitterness, anger or regrets. I release all of these things to You to today and ask You to cleanse me and fill me afresh with Your Holy Spirit. Thank You, Lord. Amen."

God wants to set people free from the mental and emotional prisons they find themselves in. Much of the battle for self-worth takes place in our minds and our souls, and it is here that we are often trapped, but Jesus is in the business of breaking our souls out of prison! Our self-image will improve dramatically as we focus on the truth that God loves us perfectly as we are. His desire is to help us to become more like Jesus as we walk with Him, but nevertheless He accepts and loves us as we are from the beginning.

Mental and Emotional Prisons

"Father, I pray today that You would break the strongholds of emotional bondage in my life and re-align my thinking with the truth of Your Word. I pray You would set me free from the lies of the enemy that have been sown in my life. Help me to meditate on

Your Word each day and to absorb Your truth into my life. Cleanse and renew my mind by the power of Your Word and the action of Your Holy Spirit. Amen."

Pray the following if you have been troubled with concerns about your physical appearance:

"Father, I thank You that You made me the way I am and that I am pleasing to You. You are happy with the way I look, so please help me to accept myself the way that I am. Help me to lay aside the things about my appearance that I often worry about, but that don't really matter in truth. Help me to remember that more important than my physical appearance is the wellbeing of my spirit. Help me to be beautiful on the inside so that I reflect more of Your glory on the outside. Set me free from worrying overly about my image. Heal me from any wounds that are hidden deep inside me due to things that people have said in the past. Set me free just to be myself before You and others, Lord. In Jesus' name. Amen."

Pray the following if you feel you lack confidence in social settings:

"Father, I pray that in all areas of social interaction You would be my confidence. I pray that Your acceptance of me would affect the way I relate to others – that I would accept myself as I am and accept others for who they are. Wherever and however the enemy has dented my self-worth and caused me to feel rejected and isolated, I pray You would bring healing and restoration. Thank You that I am valuable to You and I never need to feel unworthy or unloved because You love me perfectly. Amen."

HUMILITY AND SELF-WORTH

CHAPTER 5

HUMILITY: THE KEY TO SELF-WORTH

We've already briefly touched on the idea that comparing ourselves to others can be a trap. Often we find ourselves looking at other people's lives and situations, examining their abilities and achievements in the light of our own to see if we compare favourably or poorly. This then becomes a benchmark by which we measure our self-worth. But, of course, it is a faulty measurement. At best it is misleading to compare ourselves to others and at worst it ignores our relationship with God – and He is the only true source of our identity and self-worth.

The Bible tells us that Jesus is the author and finisher of our faith. He is responsible for transforming us into the person we are destined to become. People who suffer from low self-esteem often say things like, "I'm a nobody" or "I'm nothing." I want us to rephrase that. What we can say is, "I am nothing *without Him*."

The truth is, we are nothing without Jesus, but we are *everything with Him*! The statement, "I am nothing without Him" is a perfectly valid one that describes our ultimate value and worth in Christ, and yet does not diminish or demean us in any way because Jesus celebrates who we are. The enemy loves us to omit those last two words "without Him" and wants us to put ourselves down. But the statement "I am nothing" is an utter lie. You are not nothing, you are just nothing without Jesus! In Him you can be all that God destined you to be.

In this chapter and the next I want to look at the notion of true humility, because it holds a vital key to understanding and appreciating our self-worth.

Galatians 2:20 says,

"I am crucified with Christ: nevertheless I live; yet not I, but Christ liveth in me: and the life which I now live in the flesh I live by the faith of the Son of God, who loved me, and gave himself for me."

Paul, the writer of Galatians, used to be a single-minded, arrogant man intent on a mission to eradicate all Christians. He stood by and cheered as believers in Christ were martyred. Now, after his radical confrontation with Jesus and his subsequent conversion, he has a totally different perspective. Here he expresses as best he can the divine mystery that God's Son lives in him and through him. Paul is still alive, but he is only *fully* alive because of the life of Christ bursting within him.

Paul recognised that for all his intellectual skill and knowledge, what mattered more was this irrepressible spiritual life and power. He had been humbled and put in his place. Yet, this didn't mean that he went around hanging his head. Far from it. He energetically set about sharing what he had learnt with others, spreading the Gospel, and telling others about Jesus. Humility then, as defined by Paul's life and his teaching in the New Testament, is *accepting ourselves as no more and no less than we really are.*

At best it is misleading to compare ourselves to others and at worst it ignores our relationship with God ... True humility then

*is just being yourself, being who you are
in Christ.*

In other words, we don't pump ourselves up to sound better than we are, but equally we don't put ourselves down or make ourselves sound worse than we really are. True humility then is just being yourself, being who you are 'in Christ'.

Look again at the end of that verse: *"... the Son of God, who loved me, and gave himself for me."* Of all people, Jesus had the most reason to boast, but He never did. The Bible says that He became of "no reputation". Jesus had the most amazing credentials of any person to ever walk the planet, but He laid down who He was at the right hand of Father God and humbled Himself.

*To esteem means ... to form a favourable
opinion about someone founded on our
perception of their worth.*

The Revelation of Humility

Humility is the revelation in our spirit that we are nothing without God's power in our life. Pride is thinking that we are someone in our own strength and on our own merit.

When we accomplish something in life and attribute it to ourselves, we are not giving God any credit or glory for what He's done. Every person is born with certain gifts and abilities by the common grace afforded by our Heavenly Father to every human being. What we often fail to realise is that if we surrender those gifts to God and ask Him to empower them by His Holy Spirit, those gifts can achieve more than we ever dreamed or imagined. In Jesus our gifts and talents become all they can be and He receives the glory for it. When we hang onto our gifts and use them to our own ends, however, God is not glorified and we accomplish only a fraction of our potential.

Just as some people are overtaken by pride in their own abilities, others have a false humility that is equally dangerous. We need to be careful that by embracing the Bible's admonition to be humble, we don't go around presenting a false image of humility to others just to impress them with our self-deprecating manner. Sometimes people fall into a habit of doing this and they don't even realise they are doing it – putting themselves down in a way that is falsely modest, just because they believe it is the done thing.

The Bible tells us to humble ourselves by putting other people before ourselves. It is a choice we make to esteem others, and we can do this without needing to put ourselves down. To esteem means to have a great regard for someone, or to form a favourable opinion about someone founded on our perception of their worth. God simply wants us to recognise that everyone has worth and value, as well as understanding that we have worth and value ourselves. He wants to nurture and encourage the servant heart in us and a good way of helping us to do this is to get us to serve the needs of others and to "lift them up". When we make a point of noticing the needs of others and ministering to them, it elevates them. When we "esteem" them before God, it energises their self-worth.

Webster's dictionary defines "humility" as "freedom from pride or arrogance" and "a humbleness of mind or lowliness of mind". Elsewhere we read that humility is a "modest estimate of one's own worth". Perhaps the best definition of humility we can come up with is that it is a deep sense of our unworthiness in the sight of God, tempered with the fact that He has chosen us.

True humility brings power because when we humble ourselves God is able to lift us up in ways only He can. There is a wonderful insight into this truth in 1 Samuel 15:17. The prophet Samuel speaking to Saul says,

> *"When thou wast little in thine own sight, wast thou not made the head of the tribes of Israel, and the Lord anointed thee king over Israel?"*

There is a great revelation here. When Saul thought nothing of himself without God, the Lord anointed him king over Israel. The truth is, when we are "little in our own sight" God can lift us up. He can elevate us to high places that we would never have dreamed of achieving. We know the story and we see that Saul eventually lost the plot spiritually and it all went wrong for him. But at the beginning he knew he was nothing on his own, but could be everything with God. We must not lose sight of that for ourselves.

Seeing the Awesomeness of God

In Mark chapter 1 we read the account of John the Baptist baptizing Jesus. John sees Jesus coming from a distance and pauses in his preaching to point Him out, saying,

> *"There cometh one mightier than I after me, the latchet of whose shoes I am not worthy to stoop down and unloose. I indeed have baptized you with water: but he shall baptize you with the Holy Ghost."*
>
> (MARK 1:7-8)

We are absolutely right to be humble because we know there is One who is far mightier than us. There is One who is more powerful, stronger, more valiant and more capable than we will ever be. In the original Greek "worthy" means "fit in character or *sufficient*". I love that word "sufficient". It speaks of the all-encompassing nature of God – His ability to be everything to everyone; His ability to help us overcome in any and every circumstance. He is totally sufficient for us!

John humbles himself saying that he is not fit to stoop down before Jesus and take His shoes off – something a menial servant would have done in biblical times. In other words, John is saying, "Here is someone who is much more powerful and valiant than me. Compared to Him, I stand at less than the level of the most menial servant."

Why did John say this?

John had baptized lots of people, but he had baptized them only in water. Now here was Jesus, who John recognised from his understanding of Scripture who was going to baptize people in the Holy Ghost. He was in complete awe of what God was going to do. He knew that someone had come who was going to change *everything*!

When we take time to stand back and look, like John did, at the awesomeness of God, that's when the revelation often hits us – that He is very great and we are very small – and it helps put our life into perspective. It's good to take time to reflect on what God has done for us in the past – how kind He has been to us, how He has met our needs and answered our prayers in difficult times, or simply blessed us for no apparent reason at all. It's also good to look at the character of God and recognise what He will do for us in the future – to save and perfect us, to allow us to enjoy His presence for all eternity. This is true humility: when we see our life in the context of our great and mighty God.

So, the baptism in the Holy Ghost comes and changes everything! My own testimony is that when I was filled with the Holy Ghost my whole life changed forever! At this time in my late twenties I worshipped at the local Anglican Church and I went to the altar rail for prayer. The Lord filled me with the person of the Holy Ghost and I was "drunk in the spirit" for a week or more. The Father started to clear things out of my life: ungodly language, ungodly clothes, ungodly people. HIS FIRE HAD COME TO PURGE ME. The Refiner's fire came and I was never the same again. By the way, this was not my prayer request at that altar rail. But the Lord knew it would be the answer to all my weaknesses and the lack of holiness that was in my life at the time.

So, do you want the person of the Holy Ghost to come and dwell in you?

He is for all believers who ask (Acts 2:4) It's so simple. Let's pray:

"Heavenly Father, I see in Your Word that they were all filled with the Holy Ghost, so I ask you in the name of Jesus to baptise me and fill me to overflowing with Your Spirit. Cleanse me, fill me, refine me, I pray. Fill me with Your joy and holy boldness and please release the gift of tongues in Jesus' name. Amen."

Humility Releases God's Anointing

In Ephesians 3:7-8 Paul writes,

"Whereof I was made a minister, according to the gift of the grace of God given unto me by the effectual working of his power. Unto me, who am less than the least of all saints, is this grace given, that I should preach among the Gentiles the unsearchable riches of Christ."

What an amazing statement made by this former persecutor of believers in the Messiah! Though he was a highly educated, well-trained, intelligent man, Paul knew exactly where the source of his spiritual power was. Paul saw what a wretched state he was in before meeting the Lord Jesus, but he also knew that if he became filled with spiritual pride because of his new-found grace, he would be in an equally wretched state. God gives grace to the humble. He can use those who are humble, because nothing is stopping Him from filling them with His power.

Paul rejoiced over the fact that he had been given the grace to share the Gospel. We also need to understand the sheer privilege we have of sharing the Gospel, the good news about Jesus, with others and seeing lives changed by the power of God. But the main point here is that Paul was struck by the "unsearchable riches of Christ". He has glimpsed something of the depth and breadth of God's love and grace that completely humbled him.

Humility gets God's Attention

Psalm 10:17 says,

> *"Lord, thou hast heard the desire of the humble: thou wilt prepare their heart, thou wilt cause thine ear to hear."*

When we humble ourselves, God notices and He listens to us. Many times throughout Scripture a sharp contrast is drawn between those who are proud and those who are humble. The voice of the humble person gets heard by God, while the prayers of the proud or arrogant fall flat. Jesus told a wonderful parable about the virtue of humility:

> *"When thou art bidden of any man to a wedding, sit not down in the highest room; lest a more honourable man than thou be bidden of him; and he that bade thee and him come and say to thee, Give this man place; and thou begin with shame to take the lowest room. But when thou art bidden, go and sit down in the lowest room;*

*that when he that bade thee cometh, he may say unto
thee, Friend, go up higher: then shalt thou have worship
in the presence of them that sit at meat with thee. For
whosoever exalteth himself shall be abased; and he that
humbleth himself shall be exalted."*

(LUKE 14:8-11)

Here Jesus perfectly captures the essence of humility and
teaches us that God can work with humble people. His heart
is to lift up those who don't think more highly of themselves
than they should. In Isaiah 57 God says,

*"For thus saith the high and lofty One that inhabiteth
eternity, whose name is Holy; I dwell in the high and
holy place, with him also that is of a contrite and humble
spirit, to revive the spirit of the humble, and to revive the
heart of the contrite ones."*

(ISAIAH 57:15)

There is something so lovely in Jesus' word-picture about
being invited to a higher table. If we try to exalt ourselves,
nothing good will come of it. But if we remain humble and
place the job of "exalting" into God's hands, it's amazing
what can happen. God knows when we are ready to be
lifted up to a higher place, whether that means the level of
our anointing or a job promotion at work. He knows when
our character is ready to contain the bigger thing He has
for us.

When I was younger I was very eager to do great things
for God. I recognised that He had called me into a specific
ministry, but I had a problem: things weren't happening for
me as quickly as I wanted them to. I just wanted to get on
and see how God could use me! So I was running around
trying to make things happen and all the time thinking,

"Why aren't the church leaders letting me do things? I've got a lot to offer!"

As eager as I was to serve Him, God needed to allow me to run out of steam and arrive at the place where I was willing to submit to Him fully – to work in His way, according to His timing and to His agenda. Until I realised this, I was constantly scratching my head, wondering why, having called me, God was not opening doors for me to minister to others. If this is true of you, you probably need to face the fact that you need to die to self a little bit more. He is more concerned with shaping our characters than He is in answering our self-centred prayers.

Our own selfishness can be a huge barrier to God blessing us. Humility is not only about recognising the awesomeness of God – that's the nice bit – it is also about sacrificing our own agenda to the will of God – that's the more difficult bit. Dying to self is rarely a pleasant experience, but it is a necessary one if we are going to open ourselves up to the full benefit of the Holy Spirit working in our lives. Dying to self is not a one-off experience, it is an ongoing struggle. Paul said simply, "I die daily." We need to do the same. Every day we need to keep dying a little bit more to our selfish desires and agendas so that God can work through us, despite our weaknesses.

Humility is an Attitude We Put On

Humility is not something that anyone can pray onto us. Neither is pride something that can be cast out through prayer. We'd all love it to be that easy, wouldn't we! Instead we have to exercise our will in obedience to God. Colossians 3:12-14 speaks of an active "putting on" of certain godly attributes:

"Put on therefore, as the elect of God, holy and beloved, bowels of mercies [depths of mercies], kindness, humbleness of mind, meekness, longsuffering; forbearing one another, and forgiving one another, if any man have a quarrel against any: even as Christ forgave you, so also do ye. And above all these things put on charity [love], which is the bond of perfectness."

Verse 15 tells us what will be the result of doing this: the peace of God in our innermost being.

"And let the peace of God rule in your hearts, to the which also ye are called in one body; and be ye thankful."

We have a tendency to over-spiritualise certain things in our Christian life, whereas the Bible is very simple and straightforward. Scripture gives us clear advice about what to do and what not to do. These are certain ways in which we should behave in order to honour the Lord, Paul says, and here is a list... Make sure you "put on" these Christlike attitudes: mercy, kindness, humility, etc. The act of "putting on" gives us a helpful, visual picture, and we picture it as if we were putting on a coat, a hat or a scarf.

Humility can completely disarm others. I remember vividly conducting a series of public meetings on a ministry trip abroad. Someone told me that the local minister of the town would be coming to some of the meetings. I noticed this man the first day he came, because he was very tall. But instead of coming to sit at the front or introducing himself, as many would have done, he just turned up each day and sat right at the back of the room, taking in everything and quietly watching what was going on. On the very last day, at the end of the last meeting, he finally came to the front, but only to kneel down in front of the whole crowd of people and ask, "Will you pray with me?" The details of the prayer aren't significant, what struck me was the absolute, genuine humility of this man of God and I felt a great compassion for him.

Whenever we see genuine humility it touches our hearts. Humility is a very attractive quality. Those who are proud and arrogant can quickly overlook the humble in their superficial way. But for those with eyes to see, humility has a quiet power and grace that makes us want to be like the person who possesses it.

In the Body of Christ, especially in the West, there is too much focus on us. Often, it all seems to be about us and very little about God. We have pretty much all we could want in material terms and that works against us. We need to depend on God for very little. In other parts of the world God is moving in miraculous power, and frequently this is happening in the places where people need or have learned to depend on God much more than we do. This must be one of the reasons why we see fewer miracles in the West! A lack of dependence on God means that we deny ourselves the blessing of Him providing for us supernaturally. I think we all need to die to ourselves just a little bit more.

Each of us needs to ask God how we can grow in the ways of humility. Remember that in the economy of God, humility and brokenness equals power, because He can step in. This equation is the direct opposite to the world's view that strength equals power or knowledge equals power. No, God's power is released into a broken world when we humble ourselves, because when there is less of us, there is more of Him.

SUMMARY

- A true understanding of biblical humility is a vital key in helping us to understand and appreciate our self-worth. Humility is the revelation in our spirit that we are nothing without God's power.

- We need to be careful that we don't try to embrace humility, just because we think it is the right thing to do, as this can result in us being falsely humble: i.e. presenting a false image to others because we believe it's the right thing to do. True humility is essentially about putting the needs of others above our own, and we can do this without being self-deprecating.

- True humility results in power, because when we humble ourselves God is able to lift us up as only He can. Humility gets God's attention and causes Him to notice us. His heart is always to lift up those who don't think more highly of themselves than they should. Jesus illustrated this in a parable in Luke 14:8-11.

- Humility is an attitude that we have to deliberately "put on". We cannot pray that God will supernaturally make us humble, it is something we have to work out practically and not over-spiritualise.

CHAPTER 6

HUMILITY: FINDING THE RIGHT BALANCE

Humbling Ourselves Before God

Proverbs 22:4 says,

> *"By humility and the fear of the Lord are riches, and honour, and life."*

Here we see that two things go together well and are perfectly complementary: "humility" and "the fear of the Lord". The fear of the Lord is having an awe-inspired respect for God. It is bowing our knee in the face of His holiness, acknowledging how big He is and how small we are. Fearing God is understanding that He is omnipotent and omnipresent. Fearing God results in us wanting to live a holy life.

The facts are very clear: pride will eventually be destroyed, but humility will be rewarded with honour.

How we need a revival of the fear of God in the Church!
When a great respect for God and an attitude of humility are married together in our life, the Bible is clear about the results: riches, honour and life. God honours these attitudes and a way of life which exhibits them. And when He honours

us we see the results of His incredible favour. But the Bible also issues a warning for those who do not choose the way of humility:

"Before destruction the heart of man is haughty, and before honour is humility."

(PROVERBS 18:12)

And in 1 Peter 5:5b we read,

"Be clothed with humility: for God resisteth the proud and giveth grace to the humble."

The facts are very clear: pride will eventually be destroyed, but humility will be rewarded with honour. Scripture instructs us to humble ourselves. I can tell you from experience that it's far better to humble yourself before God, than to wait and let Him do it for you! This is the same principle Jesus was teaching us in His parable about the wedding banquet.

When we humble ourselves, God promises that at the right time He Himself will lift us up:

"Humble yourselves therefore under the mighty hand of God, that he may exalt you in due time."

(1 PETER 5:6)

This verse tells us several things. Firstly, it tells us that God desires to exalt us. He wants to lift us up and bless us. Secondly, it tells us that there is a right time for this to happen. Thirdly, it tells us that we need to leave it to God to judge exactly when that time should be. And lastly, it tells us that there is one thing that can delay the timing of God: us not humbling ourselves!

God wants to bless us, but we need to cooperate with Him so that we don't stem the flow of His blessing.

What does it mean, practically speaking, to humble ourselves before God? At the most fundamental level it is simply saying, "Lord, you know best; I know nothing!" We all have ideas, plans for our lives, schemes that we dream up that look good to us and that we think will give us the outcomes we desire in life. But the fact is, God knows what is best for us. He knows our needs better than we know them ourselves and He knows what we need to thrive and flourish in life. His heart is to give us all of that blessing and favour and more – if only we will just get out of His way and let Him do it! So often we are our own worst enemy, allowing ourselves to block God from doing the very thing that would bless us.

The next verse in 1 Peter 5 says this:

"Casting all your care upon him; for he careth for you."
(1 PETER 5:7)

So, Peter tells us that we need to humble ourselves so that God can lift us up at the right time, while casting all our cares upon Him because He cares for us. It's both interesting and reassuring that Scripture focuses in on this issue and makes it so clear, because it diffuses the very problem most of us have as soon as we hear someone advising us to humble ourselves! We think, "If I do that, then I'm in danger of not getting my needs met."

The world has a strategy that many believers have bought into: in order to get what you want/need, you have to shout the loudest. The world rewards those who make a fuss in order to get their own way. It rewards those who push themselves forward, who elbow their way to the front of the queue with little regard for the people they have marginalised to get there. We have bought into this attitude. We think that by humbling ourselves, we are somehow making our needs a lower priority for God to meet. We can't help but think that we need to shout at God to make ourselves heard and to get what we want. But actually the opposite is true: remember that when we humble ourselves it attracts God's attention. Peter is pointing out to us the fact that in the process of humbling ourselves, God takes up our cause and commits Himself to meet all our needs.

Maybe you are coming from a different angle. Perhaps you have been used to being very independent and self-sufficient? Perhaps you are used to running your own life and catering for your own needs – and you do a pretty good job of it? Certainly, it can be hard, if you are used to being independent, to see the need to constantly "cast your cares" on God. But it is so important, even if you don't see yourself as a particularly "needy" person. However naturally capable we may be, we need to see that we are always much better off when we allow God to be in charge. God will bless us immeasurably when we respond to Him in obedience and surrender to His will. His sufficiency will always be greater than ours!

> *"Not that we are sufficient of ourselves to think any thing as of ourselves; but our sufficiency is of God."*
>
> (2 CORINTHIANS 3:5)

In the Amplified Bible this verse reads,

> *"Not that we are fit (qualified and sufficient in ability) of ourselves to form personal judgments or to claim or count anything as coming from us, but our power and ability and sufficiency are from God."*

Compare this statement with the words of 1 Corinthians 1:25-27,

> *"Because the foolishness of God is wiser than men; and the weakness of God is stronger than men. For ye see your calling, brethren, how that not many wise men after the flesh, not many mighty, not many noble, are called: but God hath chosen the foolish things of the world to confound the wise; and God hath chosen the weak things of the world to confound the things which are mighty."*

Independence and self-sufficiency are values that are held up by the world as being worthy and desirable, but in God's Kingdom we are taught to rely upon the King. God's ways look upside down to the world. He values that which is weak and looks inferior to many. He chooses what the world deems foolish and worthless and then does something amazing with it.

Seeing ourselves as insignificant is a spiritual revelation. So often we have to run out of ourselves before we will submit to God and allow Him to do things His way. The strong willed and self-sufficient person may only come to that place once they have been broken, when everything in life they have established by their own hands has come crashing down. At that point we have no choice but to cry to God for help and ask Him to come in and take over – but how much better to do it before it gets to that stage.

Balanced Humility

The story of Jesus healing the servant of a Roman centurion illustrates a balanced attitude to humility and serves as a great model for us to follow. Read the following verses from Luke 7:

"Now when he had ended all his sayings in the audience of the people, he entered into Capernaum. And a certain centurion's servant, who was dear unto him, was sick, and ready to die. And when he heard of Jesus, he sent unto him the elders of the Jews, beseeching him that he would come and heal his servant. And when they came to Jesus, they besought him instantly, saying, That he was worthy for whom he should do this: for he loveth our nation, and he hath built us a synagogue. Then Jesus went with them. And when he was now not far from the house, the centurion sent friends to him, saying unto him, Lord, trouble not thyself: for I am not worthy that thou shouldest enter under my roof: wherefore neither thought I myself worthy to come unto thee: but say in a word, and my servant shall be healed. For I also am a man set under authority, having under me soldiers, and I say unto one, Go, and he goeth; and to another, Come, and he cometh; and to my servant, Do this, and he doeth it. When Jesus heard these things, he marvelled at him, and turned him about, and said unto the people that followed him, I say unto you, I have not found so great faith, no, not in Israel."

(LUKE 7:1-9)

Many Bible teachers have used this passage as a treatise on faith, and it is, but it also tells us a great deal about how to live in humility if we read between the lines.

> *We may say, "I'm not worthy", but God judged that we were worth enough for Him to send Jesus to rescue us.*

Notice, first of all that the centurion doesn't go himself to seek out Jesus, but sends representatives from the local Jewish elders. Jesus decides to go with these people and they travel towards the man's house. Hearing that Jesus is coming to visit him, the centurion hastily sends out some of his friends to tell Him, "Lord, don't trouble yourself to actually come here. I'm not worthy of entertaining your presence!"

The Centurion would have been aware of the purity issues involved with a Jew entering the house of a Gentile. Even so, he didn't consider himself worthy to host Jesus anyway, and didn't want Him to go out of His way to meet His request. Maybe he had glimpsed something of the awesomeness of Jesus' power and presence. Clearly he knew that Jesus was anointed of God to heal the sick and was being used powerfully by God. He was discerning that Jesus was no ordinary Rabbi!

Then we read that the centurion says to Jesus,

"Say in a word, and my servant shall be healed. For I also am a man set under authority, having under me soldiers, and I say unto one, Go, and he goeth; and to another, Come, and he cometh; and to my servant, Do this, and he doeth it."

The centurion's words show that he has a balanced perspective on who he is. He is humble – he recognises Jesus' status and power and responds by saying, "I am not worthy of You." But he is not simply being self-deprecating, because he is comfortable with the authority he possesses as a leader of men. He has 100 soldiers under his command and he doesn't mind ordering them about as necessary!

One of the greatest insights this story gives us is that of recognising our position in life. The centurion knew where he stood in relation to others and where he stood in relation to God. His social standing was better than many – he had servants. But the Bible reads that he loved the servant who was sick very much, so it seems logical that he didn't treat his servants badly, but with dignity and compassion. On top of that, he knew that for all his achievements he was nothing compared to God and he was powerless to help his servant without divine intervention, which he immediately sought.

A lack of self-worth could have prevented this man from seeking Jesus' intervention. He could have adopted an "I'm not worth it, so I won't ask in case He says no" attitude. Instead he found a correct balance. He said, "Lord, I need your help. Only You can do this, but You don't need to specially come and visit me – just say the word." This is faith and humility.

We have a choice to make. We need to take a balanced line in our thinking and our attitudes. We may say, "I'm not worthy", but God judged that we were worth enough for Him to send Jesus to rescue us. A lack of self-worth will have us going round in circles and we'll never accomplish that which God has called us to do. Instead, we need to learn to say "I'm nothing *without Him.*"

SUMMARY

- Humility and the fear of the Lord are complementary attributes. We "fear" or awesomely respect God because of His greatness and this results in us humbling ourselves. The Bible teaches us that these two attributes working together result in abundant blessing.

- At a practical level, humbling ourselves is simply saying to God, "You know best" and allowing Him to work in our lives in His way and in His time. God knows us better than we know ourselves and so He understands our complex needs and can meet them like no other. Much of the time we just need to get out of His way and let Him work!

- We need to allow God to bring us to a place of balanced humility, like the Roman Centurion Jesus met, who understood his place in the world and was comfortable with the boundaries set for him. He was at peace with who he was and understood what he was capable of doing and what only God was capable of doing.

WAYS TO FREEDOM

PART THREE

WAYS TO FREEDOM

CHAPTER 7

WAYS TO BE FREE AND STAY FREE

We have looked at the issue of self-worth and the various areas of life that are impacted by a lack of worth and value. We have also looked at how an understanding of true biblical humility is a vital antidote to our lack of self-worth. Now, in this last section I want to look briefly at a number of key truths that will help us to become free and remain free from issues that attack our worth and value.

Throughout this book there has been a common pattern to each of the problems that people suffer with in relation to their self-worth. That is, they all begin in the mind. The way in which we think about ourselves has a dramatic effect on our self-worth. Therefore, we must take care to constantly renew our minds with the Word of God and process our thoughts carefully.

> *God's children are not meant to live less than abundant lives, squashed and crushed by the world and its values*

In order to be truly free and to truly be ourselves, it is vitally important that we know the truth about who we are in Jesus. This essential understanding is the truth that will allow us to be the person God always intended us to be. The more we dwell on this truth and live in it, the freer we will become. There are three key areas regarding who we are in Christ that we need to focus on:

1. We Are More than Conquerors in Christ

In Jesus we can become the person God always intended us to be – the person He planned and purposed us to be from all eternity – and Scripture tells us that in Jesus we are more than conquerors.

> *"In all these things we are more than conquerors through him that loved us."*

> (ROMANS 8:37)

What does this mean for us? What does it mean for the person who struggles with self-worth and a sense of identity?

God wants us to know that we are capable of conquering in every situation in life through the power of His love. God's children are not meant to live less than abundant lives, squashed and crushed by the world and its values or suffering emotionally from the abuse of others. In Jesus it is possible for us to live in the wholeness and blessing of God. But we need to know *who we are in Him*!

Read through the following statements from Scripture that express everything that is true about you, now that you are in Christ. These are the "titles" that God has given to you as one of His children. They need to be embedded deep in your heart and mind, so that when the enemy comes throwing lies at you, trying to undermine your identity, you are ready to defend yourself.

In Christ, we are ...

... *Accepted*

I am God's child.

> *"But as many as received him, to them gave he power*
> *to become the sons of God, even to them that believe on*
> *his name."*
>
> (JOHN 1:12)

As a disciple, I am a friend of Jesus Christ.

> *"Henceforth I call you not servants; for the servant*
> *knoweth not what his lord doeth: but I have called you*
> *friends; for all things that I have heard of my Father I*
> *have made known unto you."*
>
> (JOHN 15:15)

I have been justified.

> *"Therefore being justified by faith, we have peace with*
> *God through our Lord Jesus Christ."*
>
> (ROMANS 5:1)

I am united with the Lord, and I am one with Him in spirit.

> *"But he that is joined unto the Lord is one spirit."*
>
> (1 CORINTHIANS 6:17)

I have been bought with a price and I belong to God.

> *"What? know ye not that your body is the temple of the*
> *Holy Ghost which is in you, which ye have of God, and*
> *ye are not your own? For ye are bought with a price:*
> *therefore glorify God in your body, and in your spirit,*
> *which are God's."* (1 CORINTHIANS 6:19-20)

I am a member of Christ's body.

> *"Now ye are the body of Christ, and members in particular."*
>
> (1 CORINTHIANS 12:27)

I have been chosen by God and adopted as His child.

> *"Blessed be the God and Father of our Lord Jesus Christ, who hath blessed us with all spiritual blessings in heavenly places in Christ: according as he hath chosen us in him before the foundation of the world, that we should be holy and without blame before him in love: having predestinated us unto the adoption of children by Jesus Christ to himself, according to the good pleasure of his will, to the praise of the glory of his grace, wherein he hath made us accepted in the beloved. In whom we have redemption through his blood, the forgiveness of sins, according to the riches of his grace; wherein he hath abounded toward us in all wisdom and prudence."*
>
> (EPHESIANS 1:3-8)

I have been redeemed and forgiven of all my sins.

> *"Who hath delivered us from the power of darkness, and hath translated us into the kingdom of his dear Son: in whom we have redemption through his blood, even the forgiveness of sins."*
>
> (COLOSSIANS 1:13-14)

I am complete in Christ.

"For in him dwelleth all the fullness of the Godhead bodily. And ye are complete in him, which is the head of all principality and power."

(COLOSSIANS 2:9-10)

I have direct access to the throne of grace through Jesus Christ.

"Seeing then that we have a great high priest, that is passed into the heavens, Jesus the Son of God, let us hold fast our profession. For we have not an high priest which cannot be touched with the feeling of our infirmities; but was in all points tempted like as we are, yet without sin. Let us therefore come boldly unto the throne of grace, that we may obtain mercy, and find grace to help in time of need."

(HEBREWS 4:14-16)

... Secure

I am free from condemnation.

"There is therefore now no condemnation to them which are in Christ Jesus, who walk not after the flesh, but after the Spirit."

(ROMANS 8:1)

I am assured that God works for my good in all circumstances.

"And we know that all things work together for good to them that love God, to them who are the called according to his purpose."

(ROMANS 8:28)

I am free from any condemnation brought against me and I cannot be separated from the love of God.

"What shall we then say to these things? If God be for us, who can be against us? He that spared not his own Son, but delivered him up for us all, how shall he not with him also freely give us all things? Who shall lay any thing to the charge of God's elect? It is God that justifieth. Who is he that condemneth? It is Christ that died, yea rather, that is risen again, who is even at the right hand of God, who also maketh intercession for us. Who shall separate us from the love of Christ? shall tribulation, or distress, or persecution, or famine, or nakedness, or peril, or sword? As it is written, For thy sake we are killed all the day long; we are accounted as sheep for the slaughter. Nay, in all these things we are more than conquerors through him that loved us. For I am persuaded, that neither death, nor life, nor angels, nor principalities, nor powers, nor things present, nor things to come, nor height, nor depth, nor any other creature, shall be able to separate us from the love of God, which is in Christ Jesus our Lord."

(ROMANS 8:31-39)

I have been established, anointed and sealed by God.

"Now he which stablisheth us with you in Christ, and hath anointed us, is God; who hath also sealed us, and given the earnest of the Spirit in our hearts."

(2 CORINTHIANS 1:21-22)

114

I am hidden with Christ in God.

"If ye then be risen with Christ, seek those things which are above, where Christ sitteth on the right hand of God. Set your affection on things above, not on things on the earth. For ye are dead, and your life is hid with Christ in God. When Christ, who is our life, shall appear, then shall ye also appear with him in glory."

(COLOSSIANS 3:1-4)

I am confident that God will complete the good work He started in me.

"Being confident of this very thing, that he which hath begun a good work in you will perform it until the day of Jesus Christ."

(PHILIPPIANS 1:6)

I am a citizen of heaven.

"For our conversation is in heaven; from whence also we look for the Saviour, the Lord Jesus Christ."

(PHILIPPIANS 3:20)

I have not been given a spirit of fear but of power, love and a sound mind.

"For God hath not given us the spirit of fear; but of power, and of love, and of a sound mind."

(2 TIMOTHY 1:7)

I am born of God and the evil one cannot touch me.

"We know that whosoever is born of God sinneth not;
but he that is begotten of God keepeth himself, and that
wicked one toucheth him not."

(1 JOHN 5:18)

... *Significant*

I am a branch of Jesus Christ, the true vine, and a channel
of His life.

"I am the vine, ye are the branches: He that abideth in
me, and I in him, the same bringeth forth much fruit: for
without me ye can do nothing."

(JOHN 15:5)

I have been chosen and appointed to bear fruit.

"Ye have not chosen me, but I have chosen you, and
ordained you, that ye should go and bring forth fruit, and
that your fruit should remain: that whatsoever ye shall
ask of the Father in my name, he may give it you."

(JOHN 15:16)

I am God's temple.

"Know ye not that ye are the temple of God, and that the
Spirit of God dwelleth in you?"

(1 CORINTHIANS 3:16)

I am a minister of reconciliation for God.

"Therefore if any man be in Christ, he is a new
creature: old things are passed away; behold, all

things are become new. And all things are of God,
who hath reconciled us to himself by Jesus Christ,
and hath given to us the ministry of reconciliation;
to wit, that God was in Christ, reconciling the
world unto himself, not imputing their trespasses
unto them; and hath committed unto us the word of
reconciliation. Now then we are ambassadors for
Christ, as though God did beseech you by us: we
pray you in Christ's stead, be ye reconciled to God.
For he hath made him to be sin for us, who knew no
sin; that we might be made the righteousness of God
in him."

(2 CORINTHIANS 5:17-21)

I am seated with Jesus Christ in the heavenly realm.

"And hath raised us up together, and made us sit
together in heavenly places in Christ Jesus."

(EPHESIANS 2:6)

I am God's workmanship.

"For we are his workmanship, created in Christ Jesus
unto good works, which God hath before ordained that
we should walk in them."

(EPHESIANS 2:10)

I may approach God with freedom and confidence.

"In whom we have boldness and access with confidence
by the faith of him."

(EPHESIANS 3:12)

I can do all things through Christ.

> *"I can do all things through Christ which strengtheneth me."*

(PHILIPPIANS 4:13)

When we dwell on and imbibe the Word of God, Scripture says we are being "washed with the Word". The truth of God's Word washes, cleanses and delivers us. The more we drink it in, the more its truth transforms us from the inside out. Never underestimate the healing power inherent in the Word of God, just through us reading and meditating on it.

2. *We are Crucified with Christ*

Galatians 2:20 tells us about our "position" in Christ:

> *"I am crucified with Christ: nevertheless I live; yet not I, but Christ liveth in me: and the life which I now live in the flesh I live by the faith of the Son of God, who loved me, and gave himself for me."*

As we walk with God, we need to remember that Jesus is the One who is alive in us and by faith His life flows through us. Because He dwells in us by His Holy Spirit, He can empower us to live our life according to His will. The key is, we have to co-operate with Him in order for His life and power to flow. In short, we have to surrender!

Someone once coined the phrase, "Let go and let God". Often we try desperately to cling on to aspects of ourselves that we don't want to let go of: certain habits, certain mindsets or other things. Why do we do this? Mainly because we think that if we let go of them, we will somehow lose our identity.

This is wrong! The opposite is true. The more we relinquish our "self" and its selfish motivations and desires, the more we will connect with our true identity and begin to flourish in Christ. The more we surrender ourselves to God, the more we find ourselves in Him.

We also need to surrender so that God can help us. Often we will battle with things in life ourselves while God is patiently waiting for us to call on Him for help. He wants to assist us supernaturally in every area of life. We don't need to battle through in our own strength or according to our earthly wisdom. Supernatural resources and godly wisdom are available to us. We just need to ask.

3.   We are Called in Christ

God wants to set us free because He loves us and wants us to be free in our souls. But He also sets us free so that we might serve Him. Each of us has a unique calling and a specific goal for our life. We are "called" by God for a purpose. Philippians 3:14 says,

> *"I press toward the mark for the prize of the high calling of God in Christ Jesus."*

Paul writes, "I press towards the mark." There is an aspect to the Christian faith which involves us "pressing in". In other words, taking a firm hold of that which is rightfully ours, and "pressing forward" – pursuing our God-given call. We need to press in to retain the biblical truths we have read and meditated on, and to be determined to keep the ground that God has given us in our spiritual life. If God has set us free in a particular area, we mustn't sit back passively, we need to press in and move forward to keep that freedom and gain some more ground!

We also need to press forward with what God has given us to do. God has called each one of us and gifted us for certain tasks. We don't need to wait to be given a title by someone before we start functioning in our gifts. We just need to get on with it! If God has given you a bountiful amount of compassion, then begin caring for others and helping them in whatever way seems appropriate. If God has given you a passion for intercession, then begin praying and make time for it in your life. If you are not sure what you should do, ask God to reveal to you the areas in which He has anointed you. Begin serving God wherever He has planted you – in your workplace, college, school or wherever. Ask God to give you opportunities to use your gifts and move forward.

Take Every Thought Captive

Finally, it is important that we "protect" the truth we have learned and we do this by shielding our minds from attack. The Bible calls this "taking our thoughts captive". We need to carefully process our thoughts so that we accept every thought that lines up with Scripture and is positive and nourishing, and reject every thought that is contrary to God and negative or critical. This will ensure that we nurture the truth that resides within us. We seek to protect our minds because this is where the enemy will always attack us. If he can get us confused about who we are in Christ, then he will be able to make us ineffective and we will no longer pose a threat to him.

Paul urged us to practice the discipline of taking every thought captive in 2 Corinthians 10:5:

*"Casting down imaginations, and every high thing
that exalteth itself against the knowledge of God, and
bringing into captivity every thought to the obedience
of Christ."*

120

Paul says that we must take our thoughts captive in order to prevent the lies of the enemy from undermining our knowledge of God.

We all have very active thought lives and balance a constant stream of reasoning about every area of life. Into this "stream" the enemy likes to drop stones that will divert or disrupt its flow away from God or godly things. As soon as such a thought "drops" in, Paul says we are to take it captive. The phrase literally means to "take by the spear". In other words, when a thought arrives that is contrary to God, we show it no mercy and cut it down before it has the chance to germinate and develop into an ungodly desire which will eventually lead us into sin. We are not to "mess around" with our thoughts, but quickly bring them into obedience to the Lord Jesus.

If negative thoughts regarding our self-worth pop into our head, then we can refuse to accept them, take them captive, and in response, declare who we are in Jesus. As we do that, our spirit is built up and as we repeat this truth, the Word of God cleanses and renews our mind. I encourage you to keep on reading the biblical declarations listed earlier that tell us who we are in Jesus. This will help you to undo the unhelpful thoughts you may have entertained in the past. When you have persistently gone down a particular line of thinking in the past, focusing constantly on the truth like this will help you to transform your thinking.

Conclusion

Jesus once shared a parable about wheat and tares. Essentially it is about the end time harvest, but I believe it also speaks to us about our own lives and our personal "harvest". There is much we can learn here to benefit our own souls:

> *"The kingdom of heaven is likened unto a man which sowed good seed in his field: but while men slept, his enemy came and sowed tares among the wheat, and went his way. But when the blade was sprung up, and brought forth fruit, then appeared the tares also. So the servants of the householder came and said unto him, Sir, didst not thou sow good seed in thy field? from whence then hath it tares? He said unto them, An enemy hath done this. The servants said unto him, Wilt thou then that we go and gather them up? But he said, Nay; lest while ye gather up the tares, ye root up also the wheat with them. Let both grow together until the harvest: and in the time of harvest I will say to the reapers, Gather ye together first the tares, and bind them in bundles to burn them: but gather the wheat into my barn."*
>
> (Matthew 13:24-30)

In our lives we have had good seed sown, like when we came to Jesus and we began to be changed by the action of

the Word of God. But there has been bad seed sown as well –
some we knew about and some we didn't know about. While
we "slept" spiritually, the enemy was at work in our lives,
sowing seeds that would produce negativity. Thankfully, we
are now in the hands of Jesus the victor and we are able
to overcome.

It is true for all of us that the good fruit and the bad fruit
have been growing alongside each other. These things have
grown in our soul. But there comes a season where the crops
need to be tended and, although we can see much goodness,
those bad crops need to be dealt with and pulled up.

Jesus always deals with us gently, but He is determined
that we should weed out that which is harmful to us, so that
the bad crops do not damage the roots of the good crops that
are developing. God chooses the perfect time for the tares to
be uprooted and destroyed and He works diligently at this so
that, in the fullness of time, we will produce a good harvest.

I hope that during the course of this book, you have been
able to allow the Holy Spirit to begin the process of weeding
out of your life all that would hinder your progress and spoil
the harvest. I pray that you will continue to cooperate with
Him so that an abundant harvest can be produced in your
life in due course and according to God's timing. Although
dealing with our issues does not seem pleasant at the time –
just as the tares are ripped up and burned until they are
consumed – soon the pain is forgotten and we are thankful
that we have been cleansed and healed.

I encourage you to continue allowing God to deal with
the issues in your life which affect your self-worth and don't
lose sight of the harvest which is to come.

A PRAYER OF SALVATION

Do you want God to be in charge of your life?

I tell you it is worth asking Him to be! Pray this simple prayer in faith and invite Him into your life today:

"Heavenly Father, I acknowledge You are God and I am a sinner and I need a Saviour. I thank You that Your Son Jesus died on a cross for the forgiveness of my sin, and rose again overcoming the power of death. I repent of all my sin and I ask the Lord Jesus Christ into my life that I may be born again, cleansed, made new, and filled to overflowing with the Holy Spirit. I receive You now Lord. Thank You Father for the assurance of salvation and an eternity with You. Amen."

CONTACT INFORMATION

Sozo Ministries International,
Sozo House,
Alma Road,
Romsey,
Hampshire,
SO51 8ED
UK

Telephone: 01794 522511
Fax: 01794 522577

Email: email@sozo.org
Website: www.sozo.org

In 1983 Sozo Ministries International, a healing/deliverance ministry, was birthed and decades later Marion still preaches this wholeness message. She has eight of her family working alongside her and a ministry team of people whose lives have been transformed with the message of healing and wholeness.

www.sozo.org is a regularly updated website that will help you find out all that is going on within the ministry and what we are doing for God. Information on events, meetings and conferences are all available online, as well as news sheets, free mp3 downloads and special features. Our miracle testimony section will also stir your soul! Jesus does and will heal today. The testimonies are from real people who all reached out and trusted God.

www.sozobooks.com is the bookshop and resource centre for the ministry. You will find a huge choice of books, including titles not found in many Christian bookstores. Also Marion's teachings are available on DVD, CD, mp3 and audio cassette, and all include prayer ministry for your healing and freedom.

If this book has been helpful, the following audio messages and book by Marion Daniel would complement this theme: Marion's first book *Has Anyone Seen My Father?* covers dealing with rejection and restoring our image of Father.

Message sets

What Am I Worth?

Rejection Hurts (also in a single message)

He Restoreth My Soul

Conquering Your Mind

Conquering Relationships

Hidden Abuse

Single messages

Accepted in the Beloved

Answers to Isolation

Jesus Will Take Your Shame

Confidence in Him

See our book & media catalogue or visit www.sozobooks.com for more...

A FINAL PRAYER

"Father God, thank You for Your commitment to my wholeness and healing. Today I give You permission to continue to look into my life and deal with those things which seek to hinder and block all the good You are sowing into me. Thank You for Your gentleness in dealing with me. I pray You will continue to heal me, so that I might become a blessing to many others. In Jesus' name. Amen."

We hope you enjoyed reading this
New Wine book.
For details of other New Wine books
and a wide range of titles from other
Word and Spirit publishers visit our website:
www.newwineministries.co.uk
or email us on newwine@xalt.co.uk